Reviewing Basic Grammar

2nd | *edition*

Reviewing Basic Grammar

2nd edition

Robert E. Yarber

San Diego Mesa College

Scott, Foresman and Company

Glenview, Illinois   London, England

ISBN: 0-673-16662-7

Contents

Reviewing Basic Grammar

2nd
edition

Preface

Throughout this revision of *Reviewing Basic Grammar* I have kept in mind the needs of the students and instructors in basic writing and grammar review classes. As I noted in the previous edition, a text that meets those needs should reflect the following principles:

It should emphasize the essentials of sentence structure, grammar, punctuation, and spelling, with a minimum of abstract terminology.

It should include writing because grammar and usage cannot be taught in a vacuum. The writing should be on the sentence level, where students have their most obvious problems.

It should be concise, clear, and interesting to both the student and the instructor, with abundant exercises and opportunities for evaluation.

These principles have guided the revision of *Reviewing Basic Grammar.* Each self-contained chapter features clear explanations and examples, as well as exercises in a variety of formats that require the student's active participation. The sentence-combining exercises at the end of each chapter have been revised and arranged sequentially so that they help the student develop syntactical maturity and confidence. Because of user response, a separate chapter on capitalization has been added. Further, traditional terminology continues to be used throughout the book.

Instructors will welcome the addition of many new exercises, new explanatory material, revised sentence-combining exercises, and review tests that can be graded easily and quickly.

As before, each chapter sequentially presents a complete and concise lesson in one of the common problems in basic usage and writing:

1. sentence fragments, comma-splices, and fused sentences;

2. subject-verb agreement;

3. pronoun-antecedent agreement;

4. confusion of the subject and object forms of pronouns;

5. using adjectives for adverbs and vice versa;

6. use of indefinite pronouns such as *anyone, anybody, someone, neither,* and *none;*

7. use of verbs;

8. punctuation, possessives, numbers, and capitals.

This is not an exhaustive list of all the problems that beginning writers face, of course, but it contains those errors that I have found occur regularly by freshman student writers.

Finally, another new feature found in the Instructor's Manual is a series of chapter tests available in three forms, each form equal in difficulty but offering the instructor greater variety and flexibility. Each test is easily reproducible.

I am grateful to the many instructors in colleges and universities throughout the country who have expressed their pleasure with the previous edition of *Reviewing Basic Grammar.* Several instructors offered helpful suggestions. In particular, I would like to acknowledge the contributions of Beatrice Balkcum, Wayne Community College; Alec Bond, Southwest State University; Muriel Schultz, California State University, Fullerton; June Brown, Utah Technical College at Provo; Maurice Dunbar, DeAnza College; Grace Ellis, Central Carolina Technical College; Richard Guertin, Normandale Community College; Burl Hogins, San Diego Mesa College; Pat McCormack, Itawamba Junior College; Nancy McGrath, Sacramento City College, and Joanne Podis, Dyke College.

I would also like to record my gratitude to Patricia Rossi and Carol Leon of the Scott, Foresman staff for their editorial skills and patience.

Robert E. Yarber

1

The Parts of Speech:
A Review

The English language has over a half-million words, and it is adding thousands of new ones every year. But all of these words—long or short, familiar or strange—can be divided into only eight categories: the eight parts of speech. The chances are good that you've heard of these demons since the fifth grade or so. And the likelihood is even better that you may not feel confident about recognizing them. But when you learn to recognize the parts of speech, you will be on your way to understanding how the English language works. Even more important, you will be able to identify the tools that will help you to write clear, interesting, and correct sentences and to become a more confident writer. Our study of grammar and usage begins, therefore, by examining the parts of speech.

THE NOUN

We will start with the *noun* because every English sentence either contains one or is about one. *A noun is a word used to name something—a person, a place, a thing, or an idea.*

> *Michael Jackson, Illinois, pizza, jealousy*

Some nouns refer to a general class of persons, places, or things. They are called *common nouns,* and they are never capitalized unless they are used to begin a sentence.

> *athlete, nation, skyscraper*

Some nouns refer to specific persons, places, or things. They are called *proper nouns,* and they are always capitalized.

> *John Wayne, Ireland, Empire State Building*

As you will see in later chapters, nouns are important because they can work as several parts of the sentence.

A Tip for Spotting Nouns

If you can put a word in the slot in the following sentence, it is a noun: "A (*or* An) _____ is remarkable."

Example: "An *aardvark* is remarkable."

THE PRONOUN

We couldn't get along without nouns. But occasionally, in order to avoid repetition and monotony, we use other words in place of nouns. The words that we substitute for nouns are called pronouns.

> *As Beth looked over Beth's shoulder at the other runners in the marathon, Beth realized victory was Beth's.*

This sentence is obviously monotonous by its overuse of *Beth.* We can improve it by using pronouns:

> *As Beth looked over* her *shoulder at the other runners in the marathon,* she *realized victory was* hers.

The pronouns in this sentence are *her, she,* and *hers,* and their *antecedent* (the word they refer to) is *Beth.* Here is another sentence with pronouns and an antecedent:

> *The quarterback faked a pass to his receiver before he handed the football to the fullback directly behind him.*

What are the pronouns in this sentence? What is their antecedent?

Unlike a noun, a pronoun does not name a specific person, place, thing, or idea. You will learn more about pronouns and their uses in Chapters 4 and 5. Meanwhile, you should try to recognize the following list of the most common pronouns.

I, me, mine	we, us, our, ours
you, your, yours	they, them, their, theirs
he, him, his	anybody, everybody, someone
she, her, hers	everyone, no one, somebody,
it, its	something, some, all, many, any,
who, whose, whom	each, none, one, this, that, these,
	those, which, what

Exercise 1:

Underline the nouns and circle the pronouns.

1. Loss of sleep and the rigors of the trip made her sleepy and irritable.

2. Many of the eating habits we learn as children remain with us as adults.

3. Asian cultures emphasize respect for the elderly.

4. Between you and me, the final exam was easier than I had feared.

5. Most of the laws regulating the employment of migrant workers are for the benefit of those in the fields of the Southwest.

6. Nothing is as easy as it looks, and everything takes longer than you think.

7. While they were digging in Peking, anthropologists recently discovered the remains of ancient royal burial tombs.

8. Mr. Rossi tried to define jazz for us, but he finally decided it was an impossible task.

9. If you order from a menu in a foreign language, you will often be surprised at the food the waiter brings.

10. She explained to the class the differences between communism in Russia and communism in China, but we could not understand them.

11. Several of the bystanders described the accident to us and to the police.

12. He is known as a fair and impartial referee and as someone you can respect on the field.

13. Although the Rolling Stones have produced record albums for over twenty years, they continue to attract new fans among the young flocking to see them.

14. To the relief of all of us, Jim announced the name of the winner.

15. Mr. Peerson has not told the students when he will return the tests to them.

THE VERB

Every sentence that you speak or write contains a *verb*. Sometimes the verb is only implied; usually, however, it is stated. Learning to recognize and use verbs correctly is a big step toward being a better speaker and writer.

A *verb* is a word that expresses action or a state of being and thereby tells us what a noun or pronoun does or what it is. If the verb tells us what a noun or pronoun does, it is an *action verb*.

The keeper feeds *the animals every morning.*
The Soviet Union boycotted *the 1984 Olympics.*
Lorraine collects *Pre-Columbian art.*

If the verb expresses a state of being rather than action, it is a *linking verb*. Linking verbs do not express action; instead, they connect a noun or pronoun with a word or group of words that describe or rename the subject:

A palindrome is *a sentence reading the same backwards as forwards.* (Palindrome *is linked by the verb* is *to a group of words that describe or rename it.*)

I.Q. tests are *unreliable predictors of success, according to many educators.* (Tests *is linked to* predictors *by the verb* are.)

These potato chips taste *too salty.* (Potato chips *is linked to the word that describes it*—salty—*by the verb* taste.)

He was emphatic in his refusal. (What words are linked? What word links them?)

The language of Brazil is Portuguese. (What word renames language? *How are the two words linked?)*

The most common linking verbs are formed from the verb *to be: am, are, is, was,* and *were.* Others often used as linking verbs are *appear, become, grow, remain,* and *seem,* and the ''sense'' verbs: *feel, look, smell, sound,* and *taste.*

Verbs are the only words that change their spelling to show *tense. Tense* is the time when the action of the verb occurs. Notice in the following sentences how the tense or time of the action is changed by the spelling of the verb:

Our mail carrier delivers *the mail at a different time each day.* (Present tense)

Yesterday she delivered *the mail at noon.* (Past tense)

You will learn more about the use of tense in Chapter 6.

To show additional differences in meaning, verbs use helping words which suggest the time at which the action of the verb takes place. These words are called *helping verbs,* and they always come before the main verb. Verbs that consist of helping verbs and a main verb are called *verb phrases.* Look carefully at the following sentences.

Visitors should park *their automobiles in the lot behind the administration building.* (Should park *is a verb phrase;* should *is a helping verb, and* park *is the main verb.*)

Jealousy can cause *many relationships to suffer.* (Can cause *is a verb phrase;* can *is a helping verb, and* cause *is the main verb.*)

Sara must have been using *the typewriter because it is not on the desk.* (Must have been *is a helping verb, and* using *is the main verb.*)

Here are the common helping verbs. You should memorize them.

can, could; may, might, must; shall, should; will, would

Some verbs can be either helping verbs or main verbs. In other words, if they appear alone without a helping verb, they are main verbs. But if they precede a main verb, they are helping verbs. You should memorize them.

> **be:** *am, is, are, was, were*
> **do:** *does, do, did*
> **have:** *has, have, had*

Look at the following sentences carefully:

> *The American ambassador to the United Kingdom* is *an old friend of the President's.* (Is *is the main verb in this sentence.*)
>
> *The American ambassador to the United Kingdom* is delivering *a message from the President.* (Is delivering *is a verb phrase. The main verb is* delivering, *and the helping verb is* is.)
>
> *The Parkers* have *a Great Dane.* (Have *is the main verb in this sentence.*)
>
> *The Parkers* have gone *to a great deal of trouble for us.* (Have gone *is a verb phrase. The main verb is* gone, *and the helping verb is* have.)

Tips for Recognizing Verbs

An *action verb* is a word that fits in the slot in the following sentence:
    ''*I* (or *He* or *They*) *usually* _____.''
Examples: *I usually* jog.
             He usually sneezes.
             They usually help.

A *linking verb* is a word that fits in the slot in the following sentence:
    ''*I* (or *He* or *They*) _____ *consistent.*''
Examples: *I* am *consistent.*
             He is *consistent.*
             They were *consistent.*

Exercise 2:

If the italicized word in each sentence is an action verb, write "1" on the line. If the italicized word is a linking verb, write "2." If the italicized word is a helping verb, write "3."

_____ 1. What *are* you doing?

_____ 2. It *was* impossible to avoid hitting the car.

_____ 3. The construction of the freeway *triggered* a debate among the homeowners.

_____ 4. Human blood *is* composed chiefly of water.

_____ 5. Kathy *has been* a nurse for ten years in Memphis.

_____ 6. Mike and his wife *have been traveling* in the Northwest.

_____ 7. Mail and telephone service *is* unreliable in rural Belize.

_____ 8. She *sounded* ill when I talked to her this morning.

_____ 9. Most students *were* unhappy with the new fall schedule.

_____ 10. Unfortunately, kittens *become* cats.

_____ 11. Uncle Tim *refuses* to trade his 1947 Hudson.

_____ 12. The dog carefully *smelled* the meat.

_____ 13. Clarence complained that the medicine made him *feel* worse.

_____ 14. The chef *tasted* the stew and then added some salt.

_____ 15. Margie realized she *should have been* more suspicious of the deal.

_____ 16. The attendance figures this season *are expected* to set a new record.

_____ 17. The advertiser claims that the product will make your clothes *smell* fresh.

_____ 18 The guard *sounded* the alarm when he heard the approaching steps.

_____ 19. Many college graduates *are taking* jobs unrelated to their majors.

_____ 20. Ms. Weber *has been* promoted to vice-president of the bank.

THE ADJECTIVE

In your writing you will often want to modify (or describe) a noun or pronoun. The word you use will be an *adjective*, a word that modifies nouns and pronouns. Adjectives usually answer one of the following questions: *How many? What kind? Which one? What color?*

How many? Many *countries in Africa need immediate food aid.* (Many *modifies the noun* countries.)

What kind? Financial *problems caused the price of the company's stock to drop.* (Financial *modifies the noun* problems.)

Which one? These *books were found in the gymnasium.* (These *modifies the noun* books.)

What color? The white *beaches of Australia attract millions of tourists.* (White *modifies the noun* beaches.)

The adjectives in the sentences above came immediately before the nouns they modified. Some adjectives, however, come after linking verbs and describe the subject of the verb. Adjectives in this position are called *predicate adjectives*. Study the following sentences carefully:

Hugh's eyes are blue. (Blue *is a predicate adjective because it comes after a linking verb and describes the subject,* eyes.)

After waiting half an hour, the audience became restless. (Restless *is a predicate adjective because it comes after a linking verb and describes the subject,* audience.)

Possessive pronouns (pronouns that show ownership such as *my, your, her, his, our, their*) are adjectives when they come before nouns. Notice the following examples:

our *country*

their *vacation*

my *sister-in-law*

Demonstrative pronouns (pronouns that point out or indicate) are adjectives when they come before nouns. Notice the following examples:

this *building*   these *flowers*

that *statement*   those *books*

A special type of adjective is called the *article*. The English language contains three articles: *a, an* (before words that begin with a vowel sound), and *the*.

After an *absence of sixteen years, Dustin Hoffman returned to* the *stage in* a *revival of Arthur Miller's play* Death of a Salesman.

Tips for Spotting Adjectives

1. You can add *-er* and *-est* or *more* and *most* to adjectives:
   *big, big*er, *big*gest
   beautiful, more *beautiful*, most *beautiful*

2. An adjective will fill the blank in this sentence:
   The (noun) *is* _____.
   Example: The audience is *noisy*.

3. Adjectives describe nouns and pronouns:
   The heavy *surf pounded the coastline.*
   She is lucky *that she avoided the accident.*

4. Adjectives tell *how many, what kind, which one,* and *what color.*

Exercise 3:

A. In the space provided before each sentence, write the noun or pronoun that is modified by the italicized adjective.

_____ 1. The parents of the *missing* child were interviewed on television.

_____ 2. American automobiles have had to compete with *foreign* cars within the last twenty years.

_____ 3. An injury to his elbow shortened Don's *promising* career as a pitcher.

_____ 4. Although *embarrassed* by the attention, Helen posed for the photographers.

_____ 5. The cost of living is too *high* for many Americans on fixed incomes.

_____ 6. While in New Zealand last summer, I was introduced to a number of *exotic* dishes.

_____ 7. The drawings on the walls of the cave were lifelike and *realistic.*

_____ 8. *Muffled* sounds came from the basement.

_____ 9. A *smiling* flight attendant told me that I was in the wrong seat.

_____ 10. A loud blast signaled the *approaching* bombers.

B. In the space before each sentence, write the predicate adjective that modifies the italicized noun or pronoun. Some sentences have more than one predicate adjective.

_____ 1. We soon realized that *we* were too late for the 4:00 train.

_____ 2. Although Mr. Martin was in his late seventies, *he* was still vigorous and athletic.

_____ 3. Sports commentator *Howard Cosell* is famous for his use of language.

_____ 4. The *bill* that the waiter brought for the dinner seemed excessive to me.

_____ 5. The Japanese *tourists* became confused while driving on the Hollywood Freeway.

_____ 6. The *fishing nets* were full of dark green seaweed.

_____ 7. *Jane* was nervous as she assisted at her first operation.

_____ 8. Despite the harsh comments from the critics, the *violinist* seemed delighted with his performance.

_____ 9. Harvey complained that his *room* was drafty and cold.

_____ 10. *Tina* became frustrated at her inability to hit the target.

THE ADVERB

Adverbs are words that describe or modify verbs, adjectives, and other adverbs. Study these sentences carefully:

> *The tall guard dribbled the basketball* slowly. (Slowly *modifies the verb* dribbled.)

> *The* extremely *tall guard dribbled the basketball slowly.* (Extremely *modifies the adjective* tall.)

> *The tall guard dribbled the basketball* very *slowly.* (Very *modifies the adverb* slowly.)

Adverbs usually answer the following questions: *When? Where? How? To what extent?*

When?	*Jim* immediately *realized that he had confused Jo Ann with her sister. (The adverb* immediately *modifies the verb* realized.)
Where?	*Please wait* here. *(The adverb* here *modifies the verb* wait.)
How?	*The dolphin struggled* unsuccessfully *to escape the net. (The adverb* unsuccessfully *modifies the verb* struggled.)
To what extent?	*The state capitol building was* completely *remodeled after the tornado. (The adverb* completely *modifies the verb* was remodeled.)

Adjectives and adverbs are often confused. Remember that *adjectives* describe nouns and pronouns, and that *adverbs* modify verbs, adjectives, and other adverbs. Notice the differences between the following sentences:

> *Her* loud *hiccups distracted the speaker.* (Loud *is an adjective because it modifies the noun* hiccups.)

> *If you sneeze* loudly, *you will distract the speaker.* (Loudly *is an adverb because it modifies the verb* sneeze.)

Many adverbs are formed by adding *-ly* to the adjective (as in *loudly,* in the sentence above). But keep in mind that some adverbs do not end in *-ly* (*above, never, there, very,* and so on). On the other hand, some words that end in *-ly* are not adverbs (words such as *silly, friendly,* and *lovely).*

Tips for Recognizing Adverbs

---

1. Adverbs are words that will fit in the following slot:
   "*He will do it* _____."
   Examples: *He will do it* later. *(when)*
                    He will do it here. *(where)*
                    He will do it quietly. *(how)*
                    He will do it slightly. *(to what extent)*

2. Adverbs tell *when, where, how,* and *to what extent.*

Exercise 4:

A. In the space before each sentence, write the adjective, verb, or adverb modified by the italicized adverb.

_____ 1. Jason referred to his parents *frequently.*

_____ 2. Although she smiled at us, we could tell that she was *very* angry.

_____ 3. The bull terrier growled *menacingly* at us.

_____ 4. George's chances of success are *relatively* poor.

_____ 5. Sharon blinked her eyes *rapidly* as she emerged from the movie.

_____ 6. *Exceptionally* warm temperatures caused many customers to stay home.

_____ 7. Sailors who are *too* tall are rejected for duty on submarines.

_____ 8. Some students are *rarely* seen in the library.

_____ 9. After a strike of three months, the workers returned to their jobs *yesterday.*

_____ 10. Russians *willingly* stand in lines for hours in order to buy meat.

B. In the space before each sentence, write the adverb that modifies the italicized word or words.

_____ 1. Audrey *grabbed* the telephone quickly when it rang.

_____ 2. The police officer *explained* patiently why we had to remove our car.

_____ 3. Pass-fail grading systems are particularly *popular* in difficult courses.

_____ 4. People who do not smoke or drink are more *likely* to live longer than those who do.

_____ 5. Everyone *contributed* generously to the success of the benefit performance.

_____ 6. Today, with little fanfare or ceremony, Roberta *announced* her marriage.

_____ 7. Americans *will* not *tolerate* economic justice.

_____ 8. Automobile insurance is required in nearly *all* states.

_____ 9. Because we arrived late, we were given the least *desirable* seats in the stadium.

_____ 10. Reverend Marsh *served* the congregation faithfully for thirty years.

THE PREPOSITION

Prepositions are connecting words—they do not have any meaning or content in or of themselves. They exist only to show relationships between other words. For this reason they must simply be learned or remembered. Prepositions are words like *at, by, from,* and *with* which are usually followed by a noun or pronoun *(at home, by herself, from Toledo, with you).* The word following the preposition is called its *object;* the preposition and its object are called a *prepositional phrase.*

Here are some prepositional phrases. The object in each prepositional phrase is italicized. Notice that a preposition can have more than one object, and that some prepositions are made up of more than one word.

according to *authorities*	in addition to *requirements in science*
after *the meeting*	through *the final week*
below *the deck*	together with *the coach and manager*
between *you and me*	within *the hour*
from *one coast to another*	without *a clue*

The English language contains about sixty prepositions. Here are some of the most common ones. As noted above, some prepositions consist of more than one word.

about	after	among
above	against	around
according to	ahead of	at
across	along	away from

because of	from	over
before	in	since
behind	in addition to	through
below	in front of	to
beneath	inside	together with
between	into	toward
beyond	like	under
but (when it means	of	until
except)	off	up
by	on	upon
due to	on account of	with
during	out	within
except	out of	without
for		

Prepositional phrases may serve the same function as either adjectives or adverbs in a sentence.

adjective: Rumors *of an impending attack* panicked the village. *(The italicized phrase modifies the noun Rumors)*

adjective: The ushers *in the blue suits* were college football players. *(The italicized phrase modifies the noun ushers.)*

adverb: Todd and Jan left *during the intermission. (The italicized phrase modifies the verb left.)*

adverb: The President spoke *with vigor. (The italicized phrase modifies the verb spoke.)*

Tips for Recognizing Prepositions

1. A preposition is a word that will fit the slot in the following sentence:
   "*The airplane flew* _____ *the clouds.*"

2. A preposition is a word that will fit the slot in the following sentence:
   "*I saw him* _____ *the game.*"

Some prepositions, of course, will not fit either sentence, and they must be learned.

Exercise 5:

Underline the prepositional phrase in each sentence; write ''adv'' above the phrase if it is used as an adverbial modifier, or ''adj'' if it is used as an adjectival modifier.

1. From his desk in his study, Carl could see the children playing in the yard across the street.

2. According to a recent report, one of the major causes of heart disease is lack of exercise.

3. Under the backseat of her car, Louise found the missing key chain.

4. The principal of the school welcomed the parents of the children in the fourth grade.

5. The most famous playwright during the Renaissance in England was from a small town near London.

6. One of the most important requirements of a good referee is that he know the rules of the game and enforce them impartially at all times.

7. In times of economic hardship, many of the products taken for granted by most people are regarded as luxuries.

8. By knocking on doors and studying the competition, Bob was able to exceed his sales quota during March.

9. Among the many reasons cited by the jury was the witness' inability to remember dates and names crucial to his testimony.

10. The binding of the book and the quality of the printing and paper suggested that it had been privately printed for a wealthy prince or merchant.

THE CONJUNCTION

A *conjunction* is a word that joins words or groups of words. In a sense, conjunctions are like prepositions: they do not represent things or qualities. Instead, they merely show different kinds of relationships between other words or groups of words. There are two kinds of conjunctions you will need to recognize: *coordinating* and *subordinating*.

Coordinating conjunctions join words and word groups of equal importance or rank. You should memorize these coordinating conjunctions:

and, but, so, for, nor, or, yet

The following sentences show how coordinating conjunctions join single words and groups of words:

Looters and *vandals had carried away all of the valuable artifacts. (*and links two words*)

The understudy memorized her lines, and *now she was ready.* (*and links two independent clauses*)

Is the capital of Kentucky Frankfort or *Louisville?* (*or links two words*)

You should study for your driver's license exam, or *you might fail.* (*or links two independent clauses*)

In Chapter 7 you will see how coordinating conjunctions are used in compound sentences. Incidentally, it used to be considered ungrammatical to begin a sentence with one of these words, but this "rule" is no longer observed, even by the best writers.

Some coordinating conjunctions combine with other words to form *correlative conjunctions*. The most common correlative conjunctions are *both . . . and; either . . . or; neither . . . nor;* and *not only . . . but also.*

Both *New Orleans* and *New York are major port cities.*

I will either *work next summer* or *take some math courses.*

John F. Kennedy was not only *the first Roman Catholic President* but also *the youngest President to be elected.*

Subordinating conjunctions, like coordinating conjunctions, join groups of words. Unlike coordinating conjunctions, however, they join unequal word groups or grammatical units that are "subordinate." You will study subordinating conjunctions in greater detail in Chapters 7 and 8, especially with respect to complex sentences and fragments.

Some conjunctions like *after, before, for, since, but,* and *until* can also function as prepositions:

The price of gasoline increased after *the oil embargo.* (preposition)

Small cars became more popular after *the price of gasoline increased.* (conjunction)

Dean ordered a new generator for *his car.* (preposition)

Dean ordered a new generator, for *he could not start his car.* (conjunction)

Every state but *Nebraska has a bicameral legislature.* (preposition)

Shirley wanted to tell a joke, but *she couldn't remember the punch line.* (conjunction)

Exercise 6:

Underline the coordinating conjunctions in the sentences below.

1. Woody Allen is a comic and actor, but he is also a successful movie producer.

2. Her latest album features folk songs and a Broadway show tune, yet she is best known for her operatic interpretations.

3. Neither Libya nor Cuba has diplomatic relations with the United States.

4. Because he had high blood pressure and a tendency to avoid exercise, his physician and his wife urged him to take up jogging or swimming daily.

5. I was disappointed but I tried not to show it.

THE INTERJECTION

The *interjection* (or *exclamation,* as it is sometimes called) is a word that expresses emotion and has no grammatical relationship with the rest of the sentence.

Mild interjections are followed by a comma:

No, *it's too early.*

Oh, *I suppose so.*

Yes, *that would be fine.*

Strong interjections require an exclamation mark:

No! *I refuse to go!*

Ouch! *That hurts!*

Fire!

A WORD OF CAUTION

Many words do double or triple duty; that is, they can be (for instance) a noun in one sentence and a verb in another sentence. The situation is much like a football player who lines up as a tight end on one play and a halfback on another. His function in each play is different; and so it is with words and parts of speech. A word like *light,* for example, can be used as a verb:

We always light *our Christmas tree after the children are asleep.*

It can also be used as an adjective:

Many beer drinkers prefer light *beer.*

Light can also be used as a noun:

All colors depend on light.

What part of speech is *light,* then? It depends on the sentence; no word exists in a vacuum. To determine the part of speech of a particular word, you must determine its function or use in the sentence.

1

Review Exercise

A. Identify the parts of speech in the italicized words by using the appropriate letter.

        a. noun   b. pronoun   c. adjective   d. adverb.

_____ 1. Plato said that no man is *inherently* evil.

_____ 2. Patience is *one* of the most important qualities of a good fisherman.

_____ 3. The effect of diet on intelligence has been the subject of *recent* studies.

_____ 4. Ann admitted that she had *never* read a novel in her life.

_____ 5. People in the United States live *longer* than they used to.

_____ 6. Laser beams are often used to create light shows at *rock* concerts.

_____ 7. Many divorced fathers refuse to contribute to the *support* of their children.

_____ 8. The creation of the Berlin Wall was an admission of *failure* by the East Germans.

_____ 9. *Most* of the Indian tribes have distinct, mutually unintelligible languages.

_____ 10. *Supernatural* forces were blamed for the mysterious disappearance of the ships.

B. Identify the parts of speech in the italicized words by using the appropriate letter.

        a. preposition   b. conjunction   c. interjection

_____ 11. Chuck cannot swim, *yet* he refuses to wear a life jacket when he sails.

_____ 12. Do you know the difference *between* latitude and longitude?

_____ 13. Mike wants to lose fifteen pounds, *so* he is giving up desserts.

_____ 14. Arguments *over* abortion rarely result in agreements between the opponents.

_____ 15. *No,* we shouldn't do that.

C. Identify the italicized words by using the appropriate letter.

     a. action verb   b. linking verb   c. helping verb

_____ 16. We *can* achieve these goals easily within the next week.

_____ 17. *Save* now during our year-end clearance sale.

_____ 18. The human brain *has* often been compared to a computer.

_____ 19. Shopping for a stereo *can be* an intimidating experience.

_____ 20. The number of serious crimes *has decreased* by eleven percent in our city.

_____ 21. Purchasers of gold coins are convinced that the coins *will* increase in value in the near future.

_____ 22. The repeal of Prohibition *occurred* during the first term of Franklin D. Roosevelt.

_____ 23. Many prisons *have become* training schools for crime.

_____ 24. Mr. Bagby *has* lived across the street from us for forty years.

_____ 25. Ms. Chance *has* just *bought* her first television set.

SENTENCE COMBINING

In this section and at the end of the other chapters in this book you are going to have an opportunity to apply what you have learned toward writing sentences. The technique that you will learn and practice is *sentence combining,* a simple but effective way to make your sentences smooth, interesting, and mature.

Many students write sentences that are too short and choppy or too long and confusing. Others write sentences that follow the same monotonous pattern and thereby create the impression that they were written by an inexperienced writer. Sentence combining provides ways to express even complex thoughts in sentences that are varied and effective. By practicing these techniques, you will have several options for expressing your ideas, and you will become a more confident writer.

Read the following two passages. Version "B" was written by a professional writer.

A. *The dry turf of the valley-bed gleams like soft skin. It is like sunlit and pinkish ochre soft skin. The turf spreads wide between the mountains. They seem to emit their own darkness. It is a dark-blue vapor translucent, and it makes them somber from the humped crests downward.*

B. *The dry turf of the valley-bed gleams like soft skin, sunlit and pinkish ochre, spreading wide between the mountains that seem to emit their own darkness, a dark-blue vapor translucent, sombering them from the humped crests downward. (from* Mornings in Mexico, *by D. H. Lawrence.)*

Lawrence's sentence is easier to read and understand because it uses fewer words, avoids repetition, and develops the image of the valley and mountains more forcefully. Version "A" is harder to read and follow because it is choppy, wordy, and repetitious. Although it has the same information as Lawrence's sentence, it lacks the latter's smoothness and mature sound.

By studying the sentence combining techniques used by good writers such as Lawrence, you will be able to write sentences that are forceful and clear. The techniques in these chapters will vary and will appear in the order of increasing complexity. In each case you will be asked to study a sentence pattern, combine sentences in imitation of that pattern, and write your own sentences imitating that pattern.

Sentence Combining with Prepositional Phrases

One of the easiest ways of getting rid of choppy sentences is to combine them by using prepositional phrases. On page 12 of this chapter you saw that a prepositional phrase consists of a preposition and its object, and that prepositional phrases serve as modifiers in sentences. By condensing a sentence into a prepositional phrase and embedding it in another sentence near the word it modifies, you can tighten up your sentences and avoid the choppy effect that often comes from a series of shorter sentences.

Study the following series of sentences:

1. *Sixty people attended the game. They were from his hometown. The game was at Wrigley Field.*

2. *An old man sat on a bench. The bench was in the park. He was reading a book. The book was about the stock market.*

When these sentences are combined through the use of prepositional phrases, the results are smoother, more interesting sentences that are easier to read:

(combined) 1. *Sixty people from his hometown attended the game at Wrigley Field.*

(combined) 2. *An old man sat on a bench in the park reading a book about the stock market.*

Now it is your turn to try your hand at sentence combining with prepositional phrases. Condense the ideas in the following sentence groups into prepositional phrases and combine them with the word they modify. Because there is no single "right" way to combine sentences, your sentences may vary from those of other students in your class. The goal is to write sentences that are smooth, interesting, and clear.

1. Our art teacher gave a lecture. It was about Picasso's painting "Guernica."

2. A nuclear physicist spoke to the Senate committee. He was from Stanford University. He spoke about nuclear energy.

3. A police officer gave us directions. He was in a parked patrol car. The directions were to the Museum of Modern Art.

4. China signed an agreement. The agreement was with Britain. The two nations signed the agreement last year. The agreement was over Hong Kong.

5. The population of the medieval town was reduced. The cause was a plague.

Writing Original Sentences with Prepositional Phrases

Write ten sentences of your own in which you embed information by using prepositional phrases. Underline the prepositional phrases.

2

Finding the Subject and Verb in the Sentence

Sentences are the building blocks of writing. To improve your writing you should master the sentence and its two main parts, the *subject* and the *verb.*

THE SUBJECT AND THE VERB

The *subject* of a sentence names a person, place, thing, or idea; it tells us *who* or *what* the sentence is about. The *verb* describes the action or state of being of the subject; it tells what the subject *does,* what the subject *is,* or what action the subject *receives.*

      (subject)   (verb)
The attorneys argued *over the admissibility of the evidence.*
      (subject)   (verb)
Gertrude Ederle was *the first woman to swim the English Channel.*
      (subject)   (verb)
Martin Luther King, Jr., received *the Nobel Prize.*

Each of these sentences contains a subject and a verb, and each makes a complete statement. In conversation, sentences often lack stated subjects and verbs, but their context—the words and sentences that surround them—makes clear the missing subject or verb. For example:

"Studying your math?"

"Yes. Big test tomorrow."

"Ready for it?"

"Hope so. Flunked the last one."

If this conversation were written in formal sentences, the missing subjects and verbs would be supplied, and the exchange might look something like this:

"Are you studying your math?"

"Yes. I have a big test tomorrow."

"Are you ready for it?"

"I hope so. I flunked the last one."

All sentences, then, have subjects and verbs, either stated or implied. Before proceeding further, therefore, it is important that you be able to locate the subject and verb in a sentence. Because it is usually the easiest to locate, the verb is the best place to begin.

FINDING THE VERB

You will remember from Chapter 1 that the verb may be a single word (He *sleeps*) or a verb phrase of two, three, or even four words (He *had slept*, He *had been sleeping*, He *must have been sleeping*). Remember, too, that parts of the verb can be separated by adverbs (He *must **not** have been sleeping.*)

Action Verbs

As you saw in Chapter 1, action verbs tell what the subject does:

> *The counselors teach the campers the art of survival in the wilderness.* *(What action takes place in this sentence? What do the counselors do? They* teach. *Therefore the verb in this sentence is* teach.)

> *The preacher asked the congregation to contribute to the new church.* *(What did the preacher do? He* asked. *The verb in this sentence is* asked.)

> *Visitors to the British Museum may take photographs of the exhibits.* *(What may visitors do? They* may take *photographs. The verb in this sentence is* may take.)

Linking Verbs

Some verbs do not show action. Instead, they express a condition or state of being. They are called *linking verbs,* and they link the subject to another word that renames or describes the subject. You will recall from Chapter 1 that most linking verbs are formed from the verb ''to be'' and include *am, are, is, was,* and *were.* Several other verbs often used as linking verbs are *appear, become, feel, grow, look, remain, seem, smell, sound,* and *taste.*

The verbs in the following sentences are *linking verbs.* They link their subjects to words that rename or describe them.

> *My feet* are *cold. (The linking verb* are *connects the subject* feet *with the word that describes it:* cold.)

> *Steve Martin* has become *an actor as well as comedian. (The linking verb* has become *connects the subject* Steve Martin *with the word that renames it:* actor.)

> *Your new stereo* speakers *sound great. (The linking verb* sound *connects the subject* speakers *with the word that describes it:* great.)

> *Despite having stayed up all night, Ross* seems *alert. (The linking verb* seems *connects the subject* Ross *with the word that describes it:* alert.)

Any helping (''auxiliary'') verbs in front of the main verb are part of the verb, as in the following examples:

might have *stayed*

could have *gone*

did *refuse*

should have *known*

is *painting*

may have *paid*

Some sentences have more than one verb:

The Scout troop washed *cars and* collected *old newspapers to raise funds for the trip.*

The old jalopy was painted *and its tires* were replaced *by its new owner.*

My chemistry professor collects *old bottles and* raises *goldfish.*

Exercise 1:

Underline the verbs in the following sentences; be sure to include any helping verbs. Some sentences have more than one verb.

1. The Tigers have scored thirty-seven runs in their last three games.

2. Will you be staying with your brother in Philadelphia?

3. Eddie washes and irons his shirts every week.

4. The fans booed the antics of the goalies.

5. The new owner of the company has been meeting his employees and speaking to reporters.

6. Anyone wanting to learn a foreign language must learn to think in that language.

7. Burl's closets are full of electronic gadgetry he no longer uses.

8. Scientists are predicting a major earthquake in California.

9. The bank will process and approve your loan application within three days.

10. Harriet was named a vice-president of the company in recognition of her work.

11. What do you believe is the most important invention since 1900?

12. Cindy placed her left foot in the stirrup and swung her right leg over the horse's back.

13. Mel tapped his foot and drummed his fingers impatiently.

14. The shops at the mall have been reducing their prices and offering prizes to their customers.

15. You may choose from six styles and ten colors.

Words Mistaken for the Verb

You may sometimes be confused by two forms of the verb that may be mistaken for the main verb of the sentence. These forms are the *infinitive* and the *present participle*.

The *infinitive* is the ''to'' form of the verb: *to leave, to write, to start,* and so on. The infinitive is never the main verb of the sentence. Note how the following groups of words fail to make sense because they use only the infinitive form of the verb:

Missionaries from Spain to arrive *in California in the 1760s.*

Ornithologists to study *the mating habits of condors.*

Contractors to build *cheaper and smaller houses in the future.*

These word groups can be corrected by placing a verb before the infinitive:

Missionaries from Spain began *to arrive in California in the 1760s.*

Ornithologists want *to study the mating habits of condors.*

Contractors intend *to build cheaper and smaller houses in the future.*

The *present participle* is the ''-ing'' form of the verb. It is the result of adding *-ing* to the verb, as in the following: *leaving, starting, writing,* and so on. Like the infinitive, the present participle can never stand by itself as the verb of the sentence. Notice how the following groups of words fail to make sense because they attempt to use the present participle form as their verb:

Missionaries from Spain arriving *in California in the 1760s.*

Ornithologists studying *the mating habits of condors.*

Contractors building *cheaper and smaller houses in the future.*

These word groups can be corrected by placing a form of the verb *to be* in front of the present participle:

Missionaries from Spain were *arriving in California in the 1760s.*

Ornithologists are *studying the mating habits of condors.*

Contractors will be *building cheaper and smaller houses in the future.*

A final warning: You will never find the verb in a prepositional phrase. The reason for this rule is simple. Prepositional phrases are made of prepositions and their objects, which are either nouns or pronouns—never verbs. Therefore, a prepositional phrase will never contain the verb of a sentence.

Tips on Finding the Verb

---

1. Find the verb by asking what action takes place.
2. Find the verb by asking what word links the subject with the rest of the sentence.
3. If a word fits in the following slot, it is a verb:
   "*I* (or *He* or *They*) _____."
4. Remember that the verb in a sentence will never have "to" in front of it.
5. The *-ing* form (the present participle) can be a verb only if it has a helping verb in front of it.
6. The verb will never be in a prepositional phrase.

Exercise 2:

By writing the appropriate letter on the line, identify the italicized words.

   a. verb   b. present participle   c. infinitive

___C___ 1. Doug was reluctant *to admit* that he was wrong.

___b___ 2. We *are trying* to fill your order as quickly as possible.

___b___ 3. Jack *will be leaving* for Seattle next Monday.

___C___ 4. The city council voted *to install* sodium street lights.

___a___ 5. The old man shuffled along the curb, *muttering* to himself.

___b___ 6. Smiling and *waving* to the crowd, the mayor stepped to the podium.

___a___ 7. The registrar *is mailing* the enrollment appointments this week.

_____ 8. Gordon *was waiting* for a bus when I last saw him.

_____ 9. The batter stood anxiously at the plate, *swinging* his bat.

_____ 10. Greg Louganis studied the distance from the *diving* board to the water.

_____ 11. The cable *supporting* the elevator was checked by the city inspector.

_____ 12. My financial problems *are improving* slightly.

_____ 13. Terry wanted *to surprise* his wife by coming home early.

© 1986 Scott, Foresman and Company

_____ 14. A woman who *was carrying* an armload of packages became trapped in the revolving door.

_____ 15. Clyde's *embarrassing* behavior was unexpected.

FINDING THE SUBJECT

A sentence is written about something or someone—the *subject* of the sentence. The verb, as you have learned, tells what the subject *is* or *does.* Every grammatically complete sentence has a subject. Sometimes, as in the case of commands, the subject is not directly stated but implied:

> *Please return all overdue library books by next Friday. (Although the subject* you *is not stated, it is implied.)*

The rule for finding the subject of a sentence is actually very clear. To find the subject of a sentence, first find the verb. Then ask, "Who?" or "What?" The answer will be the subject. Read the following sentences carefully to see how the rule works.

> *The invoice was paid on February 10. (By asking "What was paid?" you can easily determine the subject of this sentence:* invoice.*)*
>
> *Lou follows a strict diet because of his high blood pressure. (As in the sentence above, you can find the subject in this sentence by locating the verb and asking "Who?" or "What?"* Lou *follows a strict diet, and therefore is the subject.)*
>
> *Cracks in the plaster appeared after the last earthquake. (What appeared?* Cracks, *the subject.)*

Subjects and Other Words in the Sentence

Do not be confused if a sentence has several nouns or pronouns in it. Only the word that answers "Who?" or "What?" before the verb can be the subject. In the following sentence notice that only *mayor* answers the question, "*Who blamed?*"

> (subject)
> *The* mayor *blamed himself, not the city manager, the council, or the voters, for the defeat of the bond issue.*

Do not mistake phrases beginning with such words as *along with, in addition to, including, rather than, together with,* and similar terms for a part of the subject of the sentence. Note the following sentences:

> *The summary, as well as the chapters, contains several important terms to memorize. (Although* chapters *might appear to be the subject because it is*

closer to the verb, the subject is summary *because it answers the question* ''What *contains?*'')

The basketball players, together with their coach, are featured in this week's sports special. (The simple subject is players *because it answers the question* ''Who *are featured?*'')

Simple and Complete Subjects

The main noun or pronoun without any of its modifiers that answers the questions ''Who?'' or ''What?'' before the verb is the *simple subject*. The *complete subject* is composed of the simple subject and its modifiers—the words and phrases that describe it.

In the sentence below, ''waiter'' is the *simple subject;* ''A tall, gracious, smiling waiter'' is the *complete subject.*

A tall, gracious, smiling waiter seated us at our table.

In the sentence below, what is the simple subject? What is the complete subject?

The girl in the green dress and high heels is my sister.

When you are asked to identify the subject of a sentence, you normally name the simple subject.

Compound Subjects

A sentence can have more than one subject, just as it can have more than one verb. Two or more subjects are called *compound subjects.*

Johnny Carson and my Uncle Leo *are both from the same town in Nebraska.*

The teachers and the school board *have agreed to discuss the wage dispute.*

Either hamburgers or hot dogs *will be served at the picnic.*

Exercise 3:

Underline the simple subject of each sentence. Some sentences have compound subjects.

1. The mechanic, as well as the owner, checked the hoses and the radiator for the leak.

2. <u>Laclede</u> and <u>Chouteau</u> were among early settlers of the Mississippi Valley.

3. The fire fighters, rather than the police officers, cordoned off the street near the burning building.

4. Neither the playwright nor the producer would accept the blame for the production.

5. The construction of the Alaskan pipeline, together with changes in driving habits, helped to lessen the oil shortage.

6. Richard Burton and Elizabeth Taylor starred in several stage plays and movies.

7. Brown sugar, in addition to vanilla, should be added to the sauce.

8. Smiling at her fans, Letitia Winsome waved from the stage.

9. Dallas, rather than Minneapolis, was selected as the convention site.

10. The queen, together with her family, appeared on the balcony of the castle.

Subjects in Inverted Sentences

Most sentences follow the subject-verb pattern. In *inverted sentences,* however, the pattern is reversed: the subject generally comes *after* the verb. Read the following inverted sentences carefully:

> *Across the street stood the abandoned schoolhouse. (The abandoned* schoolhouse *stood across the street;* schoolhouse *is the subject, although* street *is in the subject position before the verb.)*

> *On my desk are two copies of his report. (What is the verb? What is the subject?)*

Questions are usually inverted, with the subject coming after the verb:

> *Was Charles Lindbergh the first man to fly across the Atlantic? (The verb* Was *precedes the subject* Charles Lindbergh.)

> *Where are the keys to the car? (The subject* keys *follows the verb* are.)

> *What is the best time to call you? (The subject* time *follows the verb* is.)

In sentences that begin with *here is, here are, there is,* or *there are,* the real subject follows the verb. To find the subject in such sentences, use the method you learned earlier. Ask ''Who?'' or ''What?'' before the verb.

> *Here is a new typewriter ribbon. (What is here? The subject,* ribbon, *is here.)*

> *There are several reasons to explain his refusal. (What are there? Several* reasons, *the subject.)*

Subjects and Prepositional Phrases

The subject of a sentence will never be in a prepositional phrase. The reason for this rule is simple. Any noun or pronoun in a prepositional phrase will be the object of the preposition, and the object of a preposition cannot also be the subject. Examine the following sentences, in which the subjects can be confused with objects of prepositions.

Thousands of tourists from countries throughout the world visit the home of Elvis Presley in Memphis, Tennessee. (Tourists, countries, *and* world *are in the subject position before the verb* visit, *but they are all objects of prepositions, and therefore cannot be the subject. By asking "Who visits?" you can determine the subject:* Thousands *visit.* Thousands *is the subject.)*

The author of Adam Bede was virtually ignored during her lifetime. (*Although* Adam Bede *is in the subject position, it is the object of a preposition and therefore cannot be the subject of this sentence. Who was virtually ignored? The* author *of* Adam Bede. *The subject is* author.*)*

One of the Beatles continues to produce records. (Beatles *is the object of a preposition and therefore is not the subject. Who continues to produce records? The subject,* One.*)*

By drawing a line through the prepositional phrases in a sentence, you can more easily identify the subject and verb. Examine the sentence below:

A congressman ~~from a district in the southern part of Florida~~ explained ~~in a recent television program during the past week~~ his reasons ~~for voting against the sale of arms to Saudi Arabia.~~

By discarding the prepositional phrases, we can easily see the subject ("A congressman") and the verb ("explained").

Tips for Finding the Subject in a Sentence

---

1. The subject will answer the questions *Who?* or *What?* before the verb.
2. In questions or inverted sentences the subject will usually come after the verb.
3. The subject of a sentence will never be "here" or "there."
4. The subject of the sentence will never be in a prepositional phrase.

Exercise 4:

Underline the simple subject once and the verb twice in these sentences.

1. Three of her sisters came from Vietnam in 1979.

2. Owners of CB radios, according to a new law, will have to secure a permit to operate them.

3. Laughing and cheering, the audience enjoyed the play.

4. After the movie we stopped at a restaurant for a pizza.

5. Would you like another cookie?

6. Many of the athletes on scholarships need tutors to pass their courses.

7. All of the windows and doors should be locked.

8. Are the standards of etiquette in our society declining?

9. Moderation in all things was a Greek ideal.

10. There are five players on each side in a basketball game.

SUBJECTS AND VERBS IN COMPOUND AND COMPLEX SENTENCES

You have seen that sentences may have more than one subject and more than one verb:

a. Mark Twain piloted a riverboat and later wrote several novels.

b. Alexander Graham Bell and Thomas A. Edison are two of this

country's most famous inventors.

c. Dwight Eisenhower and Alexander Haig both rose to the rank of

general and later entered politics.

Sentence ''a'' above has one subject and two verbs; sentence ''b'' has two subjects and one verb; and sentence ''c'' has two subjects and two verbs. All three sentences are *simple sentences* because they each contain only one *independent clause*. An independent clause is a group of words with a subject and verb capable of standing alone. As we saw above, the subject and the verb may be compound. All of the sentences we have examined up to this point have been simple sentences—that is, they have consisted of one independent clause. We will now briefly look at two other kinds of sentences: the *compound sentence* and the *complex sentence.* Both kinds of sentences are discussed in detail in Chapter 7 (''Compound and Complex Sentences''). At this point we need to learn only enough to recognize their subjects and verbs.

A *compound sentence* consists of two or more independent clauses containing closely related ideas and usually connected by a coordinating conjunction. In other words, it is two or more simple sentences connected by one of the following conjunctions:

and, but, for, nor, or, so, yet

The following are simple sentences because each contains one independent clause:

The violin has only four strings.

It is difficult to play.

By combining these two simple sentences with the conjunction *but,* we can create a *compound sentence:*

The violin has only four strings, but *it is difficult to play.*

Each of the independent clauses in the preceding sentence has its own subject (*violin* and *it*) and verb (*has* and *is*) and is capable of standing alone. A compound sentence, therefore, has at least two subjects and two verbs. Of course, a compound sentence can have more than two independent clauses. But regardless of the number of clauses, a compound sentence remains the same: two or more independent clauses usually connected by a coordinating conjunction. (In Chapter 7 you will see that semicolons may also connect independent clauses to form compound sentences.)

Notice that the conjunction *but,* which connected the two independent clauses in the compound sentence above, was preceded by a comma. In general, a coordinating conjunction linking two independent clauses in a compound sentence should be preceded by a comma. Chapter 7 will give you greater practice in the punctuation of compound sentences.

Exercise 5:

In each of the following compound sentences, underline the simple subjects and verbs of each independent clause.

1. Walter angrily picked up his briefcase and he strode briskly from the room.

2. Ignorance can usually be forgiven, but Mark's behavior is unforgivable.

3. I could not order our lunch, for the menu was in Hungarian.

4. Barbara and Emil see a movie every Saturday night, or they visit their daughter in Del Mar.

5. I studied for three hours, yet I failed my calculus test.

6. Vicki wanted to see Richard again, but he never called.

7. This coat was not a bargain, nor is it attractive.

8. Only four students enrolled in the ballet class, so the class was canceled.

9. Dorothy and Earl were married in 1927, and they have lived in the same house for all of those years.

10. One of you will have to work tonight, or we will have to close the shop.

A *complex sentence* is a sentence containing a *dependent clause.* A dependent clause is a group of words containing a subject and verb but not capable of standing alone as a sentence. (An independent clause, you remember, has a subject and a verb and *can* stand alone to form a sentence.) A dependent clause always needs to be attached to an independent clause in order to complete its meaning. Examine carefully the following sentence:

> *Before she ran for vice-president, Geraldine Ferraro was a congresswoman from New York.*

This sentence is made up of two clauses, each containing a subject and a verb. The first clause ("Before she ran for vice-president") will not stand alone to form a sentence, and therefore it is a *dependent* clause. The second clause ("Geraldine Ferraro was a congresswoman from New York") is capable of standing alone as a sentence, and therefore it is an *independent clause.* The entire sentence is a *complex sentence* because it contains a dependent clause.

You can recognize dependent clauses because they do not express complete thoughts. You can also spot them because they usually begin with a *subordinating conjunction.* Here are some of the most common subordinating conjunctions:

> *after, although, as, because, if, since, though, unless, until, when, while, why*

In Chapter 7 you will learn how to recognize and form compound and complex sentences so that your writing will have variety and will not consist only of simple sentences.

Exercise 6:

Place parentheses around the dependent clause in each of the following complex sentences. Then underline all of the subjects in the sentence once and the verbs twice.

1. Although *Star Trek* was canceled several years ago, reruns on television continue to be shown throughout the country.

2. The Lakers' center was taken from the game because he had too many fouls.

3. Although many readers do not like science fiction, they like the novels of Ray Bradbury.

4. In some cultures a baby is killed if it is left-handed.

5. Dennis always sings when he takes a shower.

6. As you have probably noticed, we planted two trees in the front yard.

7. Streetlights were not installed on the main street of our town until the merchants agreed to pay for their installation.

8. When Dr. Smith's opinion on a medical subject is asked at a party, he sends the questioner a bill.

9. As the sun sank slowly on the horizon, the owls began their plaintive moans.

10. Her grades improved because she finally learned how to study.

2

Review Exercise

A. By writing the appropriate letter on the line preceding each sentence, identify the italicized word or words.

     a. action verb b. linking verb c. helping verb d. none of the above

A 1. While in Pennsylvania, we *visited* the site of the Battle of Gettysburg.

B 2. The Beatles *were* inspired by the music of Buddy Holly.

A 3. Anyone *taking* up jogging should first have a physical examination.

C 4. Computer dating *has become* a popular way of meeting someone of the opposite sex.

D 5. Many Native Americans who live in the city have decided *to return* to the reservations.

A 6. Car pools sometimes *bring* together people of quite different backgrounds.

D 7. Mrs. Mather decided *to leave* her entire estate to her cats.

B 8. Cale Yarborough *has been* a racing car driver for several years.

_____ 9. Ashes from the volcano *had* covered the entire village.

_____ 10. Polio and measles *have been* virtually eliminated in this country.

_____ 11. The 1960s *were* a time of social unrest in the United States.

_____ 12. Our senator *voted* against the Equal Rights Amendment.

_____ 13. We *should have planned* our vacation more carefully.

B. On the blank before each sentence, write the letter that corresponds to the simple subject of the sentence. Some sentences have more than one subject.

_____ 14. Many football coaches encourage their players to study dancing in order to improve their agility and coordination.

     a. coaches b. players c. dancing d. agility and coordination

_____ 15. Body language is an important means of communication.

   a. Body   b. language   c. means   d. communication

_____ 16. One of the most annoying kinds of pollution is the noise of popping chewing gum.

   a. One   b. kinds   c. pollution   d. noise

_____ 17. Because of the success of the clothing drive at our church, fifty families
   received clothing for all of their children.

   a. success   b. drive   c. church   d. families

_____ 18. In an expensive mausoleum in Forest Lawn Cemetery was buried the pet
   poodle of the movie star.

   a. mausoleum   b. Forest Lawn Cemetery   c. poodle   d. movie star

_____ 19. The preface, as well as the summaries of the chapters, can be very helpful
   when studying a book.

   a. preface   b. summaries   c. chapters   d. book

_____ 20. The rights of the minority, as well as those of the majority, must be protected in a democracy.

   a. rights   b. minority   c. majority   d. democracy

_____ 21. Among the oldest surviving superstitions in Western culture is the belief
   in astrology.

   a. Among   b. superstitions   c. belief   d. astrology

_____ 22. There are many hobbies that can be a source of profit.

   a. There, hobbies   b. source, profit   c. hobbies, that   d. hobbies, source

_____ 23. Christianity, as well as Judaism and Islam, derives many of its precepts
   from the Bible, including the Old Testament.

   a. Christianity   b. Judaism and Islam   c. Bible   d. Old Testament

_____ 24. The laws against gambling and prostitution were vigorously defended by
   the citizens' committee.

   a. laws   b. gambling   c. prostitution   d. committee

_____ 25. Slang, as well as clothing styles, changes from one generation to another.

   a. Slang   b. clothing   c. styles   d. generation

SENTENCE COMBINING WITH COMPOUND SUBJECTS AND VERBS

In this chapter you saw that sentences may have more than one subject and verb. When short sentences have the same subject or verb, they can often be combined into longer, smoother simple sentences.

Notice how the following pairs of sentences have been effectively combined into longer sentences.

1. French "new wave" films have influenced American taste and culture.
   British "punk rock" music has influenced American taste and culture.

Because these sentences have *different* subjects but the *same* verb, they can be combined into one longer sentence with the help of a coordinating conjunction:

(combined) French "new wave" films and British "punk rock" music have influenced American taste and culture.

2. Sam took the telephone off the hook. He sat in his easy chair. He took a nap.

Because these sentences are about the *same* subject doing several things, they can be combined into one longer sentence:

(combined) Sam took the telephone off the hook, sat in his easy chair, and took a nap.

3. Marcella ate her meal in silence and stared out the window.
   Lee ate his meal in silence and stared out the window.

This pair of sentences offers a slightly different combination: two *different* subjects are doing the *same* two things. As in the case of the sentence in "1" and "2" above, they can be combined by using coordinating conjunctions:

(combined) Marcella and Lee ate their meals in silence and stared out the window.

Using the techniques presented above, combine the following pairs of sentences with compound subjects or verbs.

1. Dolores has a new microwave oven. She uses it to prepare quick meals.

2. The driver honked his horn. He applied his brakes. He tried to avoid the pedestrians.

3. Harold called on registered voters. He made telephone calls. He urged his friends to vote for Senator Wilson.

4. Luis was born in Sonora, Mexico. Alvaro was also born in Sonora. They own a jewelry store downtown.

5. The Hungarian border authorities wanted to see our visas. The Polish
   authorities wanted to see our visas.

Writing Original Sentences with Compound Subjects or Verbs

Write ten sentences of your own with compound subjects or verbs (or both). Underline all subjects once and underline all verbs twice.

3

Making the Subject and Verb Agree

Mistakes in subject-verb agreement are among the most common writing errors, and they are particularly irritating to readers. The rule on subject-verb agreement is obvious:

The subject and the verb must agree in number and in person.

Agreement in number means that a singular subject takes a singular verb and a plural subject takes a plural verb. The singular form of all verbs except *be* and *have* ends in *-s* or *-es: goes, takes, writes, fishes, brings, drives.* The singular forms of *be* and *have* are *is* and *has.* The singular form of the verb is used when the subject is *he, she, it,* a singular indefinite pronoun (such as *anyone* or *somebody*), or a singular noun. Plural verbs do not have these endings, and they are used when the subject is *I, you, we, they,* or a plural noun.

A singular subject with a singular verb:

Howard's dog barks *like a seal.*

A plural subject with a plural verb:

All recruits *in our police department* attend *classes in race relations.*

Notice that adding an *-s* or *-es* to a noun makes the noun *plural,* but adding *-s* or *-es* to a verb in the present tense makes the verb *singular.*

Agreement in person means that a subject and its verb must both be in the same person (*first, second,* and *third*). The following sentences illustrate this rule.

First person (I, we)

I stay *[not* stays*] out of direct sunlight as much as possible because I* get *[not* gets*] sunburned easily.*

We stay *[not* stays*] in a condominium near Aspen when we* take *[not* takes*] our vacation.*

Second person (you)

You are *[not* be *or* is*] much taller than your sister.*

You boys deserve *[not* deserves*] recognition for the fine work that all of you* have *[not* has*] done.*

Third person (he, she, it, they)

John McEnroe irritates *[not* irritate*] his opponents because he* takes *[not* take*] extra time between serves.*

Al and Myra want *[not* wants*] to get married next month. They* are *[not* is*] very excited.*

Exercise 1:

Circle the verbs that can be used with the following subjects. There may be more than one verb.

Example: *She   bring, (walks,) study, (plays)*

1. I   sings, counts, feel, stay

2. You   accepts, touch, aims, ask

3. They   arrive, appeals, keep, leaps

4. The dog   sleep, barks, eats, run

5. We   helps, hope, need, takes

6. The tourists   worries, smile, offers, own

7. She   eat, discusses, grows, have

8. My parents   travels, gives, tell, weighs

9. He   knows, skate, sings, treat

10. It   takes, believes, show, goes

If the rule given above is so simple, why are there so many errors in subject-verb agreement? Probably because of the writer's uncertainty about the identity of the real subject of the sentence and confusion about whether the subject and verb are singular or plural.

Here are three steps to ensure subject-verb agreement. *First,* find the subject of the sentence. (You may want to review Chapter 2.) *Second,* determine whether the subject is singular or plural. *Third,* select the appropriate singular or plural form of the verb to agree with the subject. The suggestions below will help you follow these steps.

1. Remember that a verb must agree with its subject, not with any words that follow the subject but are not part of it. These include terms like *as well as, including, such as, along with, accompanied by,* and *rather than.* If the subject is singular, use a singular verb; if the subject is plural, use a plural verb.

    A taped confession by the suspects, as well as statements by eyewitnesses, has *[not* have*] been read to the jury.*

    The color of the container, not the contents or advertising claims, usually determines *[not* determine*] the buyer's initial reaction to a product.*

    Plans for the convention center, together with a proposal for a tax increase, are *[not* is*] to be presented to the aldermen today.*

    The ambassadors from the South American countries, accompanied by a translator, intend *[not* intends*] to meet with the President this afternoon.*

2. Don't confuse the subject with words that rename it in the sentence.

    The police officer's only reward was *[not were] threats and taunts.*
    The cause of the accident was *[not were] the faulty brakes.*
    The attorney's secretaries are *[not is] the source of the news leak.*

3. Don't be confused by sentences that are not in the usual subject-verb pattern.

    Where is *[not are] the box of paper clips that were on my desk?*
    Are [not Is] cumulus clouds a sign of rain?

    Under the sofa were *[not was] found the missing cufflinks.*
    BUT: Under the sofa was *[not were] the set of missing cufflinks.*

    There are *[not is] many reasons for her success.*
    There is *[not are] one particular reason for her success.*

Exercise 2:

Draw a line under the simple or compound subject. Then choose the correct verb and write the appropriate letter in the blank.

_____ 1. The beneficiary of the insurance policy (a. was   b. were) Betty, as well as her children.

_____ 2. News anchors, rather than the story, often (a. receive   b. receives) the viewers' attention.

_____ 3. On the hook (a. hang   b. hangs) several clothing bags.

_____ 4. In the evening (a. come   b. comes) the final rounds of the meet.

_____ 5. (a. Has   b. Have) the trains for New Haven left yet?

_____ 6. A problem facing our community (a. are   b. is) mosquitoes.

_____ 7. Tourists (a. are   b. is) a source of income for Miami.

_____ 8. Through the clouds (a. was   b. were) seen the summer moon.

_____ 9. The foul odors (a. cause   b. causes) nausea.

_____ 10. There (a. are   b. is) a good reason for the many auto fatalities at that intersection.

4. Subjects connected by "and" or by "both . . . and" usually require a plural verb.

Following the proper diet and *getting enough exercise* are *important for maintaining one's health.*

Both *William Faulkner* and *Saul Bellow* have *received the Nobel Prize for Literature.*

Exceptions: Use a singular verb when a compound subject refers to the same person or thing:

Vinegar and oil is *my favorite salad dressing.*

The secretary and treasurer of our class last year was *Arlene Kukla.*

Use a singular verb when a compound subject is preceded by *each, every, many a,* or *many an:*

Each *owner and tenant* has *been given a copy of the new zoning regulations.*

Every *cable and pulley* receives *a monthly inspection.*

Use a plural verb when a compound subject is followed by *each:*

The tenor and the soprano each wear *different costumes in the final act.*

5. If the subject consists of two or more words connected by *or, either . . . or, neither . . . nor,* or *not only . . . but also,* the verb agrees with the subject that is closer to it. This rule presents few problems when both subjects are plural or singular:

Neither *the politicians* nor *the voters* show *much interest in this year's election. (Both subjects are plural, and therefore the verb is plural.)*

Not only *the car* but also *the greenhouse* was *damaged by the hailstorm. (Both subjects are singular, and therefore the verb is singular.)*

When one part of the subject is singular and the other is plural, the verb agrees with the part that is closer to it:

Either *the frost* or *the aphids* have *killed my roses. (The plural noun* aphids *is closer to the verb, and therefore the verb is plural.)*

Sentences with singular and plural subjects usually sound better with plural verbs. Notice the difference between the following sentences.

Neither the players nor the coach likes *the new rules. (Although technically correct, this sentence would sound less awkward if the subjects were reversed and a plural verb used.)*

Neither the coach nor the players like *the new rules. (This version is less awkward and has not sacrificed the meaning of the sentence.)*

Remember . . .

---

1. Adding an *-s* or *-es* to a *noun* makes the noun *plural.*
   Adding an *-s* or *-es* to a *verb* makes the verb *singular.*
2. If the subject is singular, the verb must be singular;
   if the subject is plural, the verb must be plural.
3. The verb must agree with its *subject,* not with any other words in the sentence.
   Don't be confused by sentences not in the usual subject-verb pattern.

Exercise 3:

Write the letter of the correct verb on the line.

_____ 1. Since childhood, my best friend and confidant (a. has   b. have) been my older brother.

_____ 2. Both local elections and the presidential race (a. stimulate   b. stimulates) an interest in politics.

_____ 3. My childhood model and hero (a. was   b. were) the Lone Ranger.

_____ 4. Children and the elderly (a. are   b. is) the chief beneficiaries of welfare payments.

_____ 5. Bread and water (a. was   b. were) the prisoner's only meal.

_____ 6. Either cookies or cake (a. are   b. is) available for dessert.

_____ 7. Neither Dale nor Jesse (a. admit   b. admits) that the door was left unlocked.

_____ 8. Every bank and savings institution (a. offer   b. offers) a variety of inducements to the investor.

_____ 9. Mr. Valdez and his wife each (a. play   b. plays) the organ at their church.

_____ 10. Many a promise to college athletes (a. has   b. have) been broken.

6. Indefinite pronouns that are singular take singular verbs, and indefinite pronouns that are plural take plural verbs. Some pronouns may be either singular or plural in meaning, depending on the noun or pronoun they refer to. An indefinite pronoun is one that does not refer to a specific thing or person.

When used as subjects or as adjectives modifying subjects, the following indefinite pronouns are always singular and take singular verbs:

another	many a
anybody	much
anyone	neither
anything	nobody
each	no one
each one	nothing
either	one
every	other
everybody	somebody
everyone	something
everything	someone

Everybody is *eligible for the drawing tonight.*
Much of the work on the engine has *been done.*
Something tells *me that I am wrong.*
Each dismissed worker receives *two weeks' pay.*

When used as subjects or as adjectives modifying subjects, the following indefinite pronouns are always plural and take plural verbs:

both	others
few	several
many	

Few of the passengers on the last cruise of the Titanic are *living today.*
Many of the parts in an American car are *manufactured in other countries; several* come *from Japan.*

When used as subjects or as adjectives modifying subjects, the following indefinite pronouns may be singular or plural, depending on the nouns or pronouns they refer to:

all	most
any	none
more	some

Unfortunately, all of the rumors were *true.*
All of the snow has *melted.*

Most of the music sounds *like Crosby, Stills and Nash.*

Most of my freckles have *disappeared.*

NOTE: *None* is considered a singular pronoun in formal usage. According to informal usage, however, it may be singular or plural, depending on the noun it refers to. Note the difference in the following sentences:

(formal usage)   None of the roses *has* bloomed yet.
(informal usage)   None of the roses *have* bloomed yet.

Exercise 4:

On the line in front of each sentence write the letter corresponding to the correct verb.

_____ 1. Everyone, including the winners, (a. admit   b. admits) that the judges were biased.

_____ 2. Anyone turning in canned goods (a. receive   b. receives) a free ticket to the concert.

_____ 3. All of the chemicals (a. was   b. were) labeled and placed on their shelves.

_____ 4. Some of the suspicion expressed by the long-time residents (a. has   b. have) faded away.

_____ 5. The preacher claimed that everyone, even atheists, (a. believes   b. believe) in something.

_____ 6. Most of the homes in the new subdivision (a. has   b. have) been bought by young couples.

_____ 7. Gene complained that none of the orders (a. has   b. have) been delivered yet.

_____ 8. Each of the committee members (a. vote   b. votes) by secret ballot.

_____ 9. Everything in the room, including the table and chairs, (a. was   b. were) painted white.

_____ 10. Nobody except the custodians (a. has   b. have) a key to the building.

Remember . . .

Some indefinite pronouns always take *singular* verbs; some always take *plural* verbs; still other indefinite pronouns may be singular *or* plural, depending on the nouns or pronouns they refer to. Look over the lists on page 45 if you are not sure.

---

7. If the subject is *who, which,* or *that,* be careful: all of these relative pronouns can be singular or plural, depending on their antecedents. When one of them is the subject, its verb must agree with its antecedent in number.

Rick is one of those musicians who are *able to play music at first sight.* (Who *refers to* musicians; *several musicians are able to play music at first sight, and Rick is one of them.*)

Lee is the only one of the musicians who has *forgotten his music.* (Who *refers to* one. *Among the musicians, only one, Lee, has forgotten his music.*)

I ordered one of the typewriters that were *on sale.* (That *refers to* typewriters *and therefore takes a plural verb.*)

I also bought a desk that was *reduced forty percent.* (That *refers to* desk *and therefore takes a singular verb.*)

Exercise 5:

On the line in front of each sentence write the letter corresponding to the correct verb.

_____ 1. Jan is the only swimmer on the team who (a. swim   b. swims) with her eyes closed.

_____ 2. Our cafeteria is one of the few that (a. make   b. makes) a profit.

_____ 3. Kathy is the only child in the family who (a. live   b. lives) at home.

_____ 4. Ours is one of the neighborhoods that (a. was   b. were) featured in the newspaper.

_____ 5. John Milton is a writer who (a. present   b. presents) problems to the casual reader.

_____ 6. Marcia is the only waitress who (a. work   b. works) part-time.

_____ 7. Collecting antiques is one of the hobbies that (a. require   b. requires) a knowledge of history.

_____ 8. Mel is the only one of the musicians who (a. has   b. have) gone to a music conservatory.

_____ 9. Dr. Elton's study is the only report that (a. criticize   b. criticizes) the results of the experiment.

_____ 10. Japan is one of the nations that (a. relies   b. rely) on imported fuel.

8. Collective nouns take singular verbs when the group is regarded as a unit, and plural verbs when the individuals of the group are regarded separately.

A *collective noun* is a word singular in form but referring to a group of people or things. Some common collective nouns are *army, assembly, committee, company, couple, crowd, faculty, family, flock, group, herd, jury, pair, squad,* and *team.*
When the group is thought of as acting as one unit, the verb should be singular.

The faculty is *happy that its request for additional secretarial help has been granted.*

The committee has *published the list of witnesses who will appear.*

The couple was *married last week.*

If the members of the group are thought of as acting separately, the verb should be plural.

The faculty have *been assigned their offices and parking spaces.*

The committee are *not able to agree on the winner.*

The couple constantly argue *over their jobs and their children.*

9. Some nouns appear plural in form but are usually singular in meaning and therefore require singular verbs. The following nouns are used this way: *athletics, economics, electronics, mathematics, measles, mumps, news, physics, politics, statistics.*

Mathematics frightens *many students.*

The news from the doctor is *encouraging.*

Politics is *the art of the possible.*

When the items they refer to are plural in meaning, these words are plural.

The economics of your plan sound *reasonable.*

The statistics indicate *that little progress has been made.*

10. Subjects plural in form that indicate a quantity or number take a singular verb if the subject is considered a unit but a plural verb if the individual parts of the subject are regarded separately. Such expressions include *one-half of* (and other fractions), *a part of, a majority of,* and *a percentage of.*
   If a singular noun follows *of* or is implied, use a singular verb:

Two-thirds of his fortune consists *of real estate.*

Part of our intelligence, according to geneticists, depends *on our genes.*

A majority of the herd of cattle has *to be destroyed.*

If a plural noun follows *of* or is implied, use a plural verb:

Three-fourths of the students in the third grade speak *a foreign language.*

A percentage of our individual characteristics come *from our genes.*

A majority of the lawyers want *to make the law exam more difficult.*

11. Words that refer to distance, amounts, and measurements require singular verbs when they represent a total amount. When they refer to a number of individual items, they require plural verbs.

   Over twenty thousand dollars was *spent on the renovation of the old house.*

   Many thousands of dollars were *lost in gambling.*

   Two miles is *the maximum range of his new rifle.*

   The last two miles were *paved last week.*

   Six months is *a long time to wait for an answer.*

   Six months have *passed since we last heard from you.*

12. When *the number* is used as the subject, it requires a singular verb. *A number* is always plural.

   The number of students who have to work part-time is *increasing.*

   A number of students receive *financial support from their parents.*

Remember . . .

Collective nouns take singular verbs if you consider the group as a unit; they take plural verbs if you regard the individuals in the group separately.

A number **are,** but *the number* **is.**

Exercise 6:

On the line in front of each sentence write the letter corresponding to the correct verb.

_____ 1. The sophomore class (a. want   b. wants) to go to Disneyland during the spring break.

_____ 2. One-half of the questions (a. were   b. was) about the candidate's finances.

_____ 3. The number of boats in the harbor (a. present   b. presents) a problem to the arriving Navy ships.

_____ 4. A number of jobs that were advertised by the company (a. remain   b. remains) available.

_____ 5. The faculty at the seminary (a. tend   b. tends) to be conservative in their religious beliefs.

_____ 6. The last six miles (a. was   b. were) paved by the county road department.

_____ 7. Statistics (a. reveal   b. reveals) that women are still paid less than men for doing the same work.

_____ 8. Over two-thirds of last year's college graduates (a. has   b. have) admitted that they cheated in college.

_____ 9. My advisor said that statistics (a. are   b. is) a required course for psychology majors.

_____ 10. We decided that two hours (a. was   b. were) too long to wait for a table at the restaurant.

_____ 11. About half of the dogs at the pound (a. are   b. is) of unrecognizable breed.

_____ 12. Approximately $450 (a. remain   b. remains) in the club's account.

_____ 13. Twenty-six miles (a. are   b. is) the distance for the marathon next weekend.

_____ 14. Every year the board of directors of most companies (a. distribute b. distributes) a report of earnings to the stockholders.

_____ 15. The couple (a. was   b. were) honored at an anniversary dinner at the local church.

3

NAME   DATE

Review Exercise

On the line preceding each question, write the letter corresponding to the correct answer.

_____ 1. All of the following pronouns are third person *except:*
       a. I b. he c. she d. they

_____ 2. All of the following statements are true *except:*
    a.   The singular form of the verb is used when the subject is *he, she, it.*
    b.   Plural verbs are used when the subject is *I, you, we, they.*
    c.   Adding an *-s* or *-es* to a noun makes the noun plural.
    d.   Adding an *-s* or *-es* to a verb in the present tense makes the verb plural.

_____ 3. Which of the following verbs cannot be used with the subject *They:*
       a. stay b. remain c. leaves d. bring

__b__ 4. The language of Brazil and Portugal (a. are b. is) Portuguese.

__a__ 5. Some of the animals in the kennel (a. suffer b. suffers) from abuse.

__b__ 6. In the stadium (a. was b. were) over sixty thousand fans.

__a__ 7. London, as well as Berlin, (a. has b. have) hosted the Olympic games.

__b__ 8. A fee of ten dollars (a. are b. is) required for the fishing license.

__a__ 9. Jack's wallet, along with his identification papers and credit cards, (a. was b. were) stolen from his locker last night.

__a__ 10. A Russian diplomat, together with his wife and children, (a. has b. have) taken refuge in the Canadian embassy.

__a__ 11. Fred Chance is one of those salespeople who (a. create b. creates) their own opportunities.

__b__ 12. Some of the coal in the strip mines (a. remain b. remains) inaccessible.

__a__ 13. The reason for the acquittal (a. was b. were) the strong closing arguments of the defense attorney.

__b__ 14. The labor, not the parts, (a. are b. is) expensive.

© 1986 Scott, Foresman and Company

51

_b_ 15. Sociology is the only one of my subjects that (a. meet   b. meets) on Friday.

_b_ 16. Everyone who (a. register   b. registers) is eligible for a door prize.

_a_ 17. Either Mickey or the boys (a. intend   b. intends) to call this evening.

_a or b_ 18. The jury (a. come   b. comes) from diverse ethnic and social backgrounds.

_a_ 19. Geraniums are one of those flowers that (a. require   b. requires) little attention.

_a_ 20. An air conditioner, as well as three filing cabinets, (a. was   b. were) purchased for Ms. Howard's office.

_b_ 21. Every June the Queen of England, accompanied by several dignitaries and staff members, (a. review   b. reviews) the Coldstream Guards.

_a_ 22. The lifeguard's only fear (a. was   b. were) the riptides that appeared without warning.

_b_ 23. The source of the country's wealth (a. are   b. is) its gold mines.

_a_ 24. Under the rosebush in the garden (a. are   b. is) buried the coins.

_b_ 25. My history teacher and adviser, Dr. McIver, (a. wear   b. wears) kilts and plays the bagpipes.

SENTENCE COMBINING WITH COMPOUND SENTENCES

Two or more short sentences can often be combined to form a compound sentence. In Chapter 2 you saw that a compound sentence consists of two or more independent clauses containing closely related ideas, and that the clauses are usually connected by one of the following coordinating conjunctions: *and, but, for, nor, or, so, yet.*

When a coordinating conjunction is used to connect independent clauses, it is usually preceded by a comma:

> *Many critics have attacked the public schools*, but *no one seems to have any solutions.*

A semicolon may also be used to connect independent clauses to form compound sentences:

> *Albert went to Las Vegas with high hopes*; he *returned, full of dejection.*

Sentence combining with compound sentences is appropriate when the ideas in both independent clauses are on the same level and of the same importance. The danger in such sentences is that they can become monotonous: ''We left Jonesboro at nine in the morning, and we had breakfast at Carbondale, and then we drove nonstop to Springfield, and we stopped for gas in Joliet, and we arrived in Downers Grove at six o'clock.'' The antidote to such sentences is to use a variety of conjunctions, as well as the semicolon and conjunctive adverbs.

Notice how the following short sentences are combined:

1. Joan was angry. She let everyone know it.
(combined)   Joan was angry, *and* she let everyone know it.

2. State your reasons now. Forever hold your peace.
(combined)   State your reasons now, *or* forever hold your peace.

3. Mr. Gildred is seventy-six years old. He still plays tennis daily.
(combined)   Mr. Gildred is seventy-six years old, *but* he still plays tennis daily.

4. The king would not meet with parliament. He would not acknowledge its authority.
(combined)   The king would not meet with parliament, *nor* would he acknowledge its authority.

5. Patricia and her husband love North Carolina. They miss their families in New York.
(combined)   Patricia and her husband love North Carolina, *but* they miss their families in New York.

By using coordinating conjunctions, semicolons, and conjunctive adverbs, combine the following groups of sentences. Remember to put a comma before a coordinating conjunction when it links two independent clauses.

1. Rosalind wore eyeglasses for several years. Now she wears contact lenses.

2. Darkness posed a problem for the explorers. Choking clouds of dust were the main obstacle.

3. Our eyes seem to focus on an entire scene all at one time. This is a misconception.

4. All aircraft feature no-smoking and smoking sections. At times, there may not be sufficient seating in the section you prefer.

5. Life is full of hard choices. Some are more difficult than others.

Writing Original Compound Sentences

Write ten original compound sentences. If you use a coordinating conjunction to connect independent clauses, be sure to insert a comma before it.

4

Using the Correct Form of the Pronoun

Most of us—unless we were just beginning to learn the English language or were babies—would not be likely to say or write sentences like ''Me am tired'' or ''Her is my sister.'' We instinctively know that ''I'' is the subject for ''am'' and that ''She'' is used with ''is.'' Unfortunately, the choices we face in our writing and speaking are not always so obvious. For example, do we say ''between you and I'' or ''between you and me''? What about ''he and myself''? Is there any way to keep ''who'' and ''whom'' separate? Pronouns can cause a great deal of uncertainty, even among the most educated speakers and writers.

One probable reason for confusion over pronouns is the existence of so many classes and forms to choose from. Unlike prepositions or conjunctions and most other parts of speech, pronouns have the distracting habit of changing their form or spelling depending on the way they are used in a particular sentence. To use them with confidence, therefore, it is important to recognize the various kinds of pronouns and to learn the specific way each kind is used in a sentence.

We will begin our study of this confusing part of speech with an overview of the most important classes of pronouns and then examine them more closely.

THE CLASSES OF PRONOUNS

Pronouns can be classified according to their form (the way they are spelled) and their function (the way they are used in a sentence).

1. Personal pronouns *(I, you, he, she, it, we, they)*

Personal pronouns refer to specific individuals, and they are the pronouns most frequently used in writing and speaking. Personal pronouns can be singular or plural, and they can be classified by *gender (masculine, feminine,* or *neuter)* and by *function* or *case (subjective, possessive,* and *objective).*

2. Indefinite pronouns *(all, anybody, anyone, anything, both, each, either, everybody, some, somebody)*

Although they function as nouns, indefinite pronouns do not refer to specific individuals. Because of their importance in pronoun agreement and reference, they are treated in detail in Chapter 5 (''Common Errors in Pronoun Agreement and Reference'').

3. Demonstrative pronouns *(this, that, these, those)*

Demonstrative pronouns point out persons or things, as in the following:

This *is the house I was born in.* Those *are the trees my father planted.*

4. **Relative pronouns** *(who, which, that)*

These pronouns connect or relate groups of words to nouns or other pronouns, as in the following sentence:

A Vietnam veteran who *is suffering from cancer testified* that *it was caused by chemicals* which *were used during the war.*

Because relative pronouns are used to introduce dependent clauses in complex sentences, they are discussed in Chapter 7 (''Compound and Complex Sentences'').

5. **Intensive pronouns** *(myself, ourselves, yourself, yourselves,* and other personal pronouns plus *-self* or *-selves.)*

Intensive pronouns strengthen or intensify the subject of a verb:

I did it myself.

You yourself *are guilty.*

6. **Reflexive pronouns** (Like intensive pronouns, these are formed by a personal pronoun plus *-self* or *-selves*.)

Reflexive pronouns are used to direct the action of a verb toward its subject:

He helped himself *to the cake.*

They let themselves *into the apartment.*

7. **Interrogative pronouns** *(who, which, what, whoever, whatever, whose)*

These pronouns introduce questions:

Who *knows the answer?*

Whose *is this?*

What *is the anticipated population of the United States in 1999?*

Because personal pronouns are used most often—and because they cause most of the problems in pronoun usage—we will begin with them.

PERSONAL PRONOUNS

The Subject Pronouns *(I, you, he, she, it, who, whoever, we, they)*

Subject pronouns are used as the *subject of a verb*, as a *subject complement*, or as an *appositive identifying a subject*.

AS THE SUBJECT OF A VERB:

Mac and I [not me] rowed until we were exhausted.

Either she or I [not her or me] can explain the equation to you.

NOTE: In some sentences a pronoun will be the subject of an implied verb. This occurs often in comparisons introduced by *than* or *as.* In such cases the subject form of the pronoun should be used. In the following sentences, the implied verbs are in parentheses.

He is fourteen pounds heavier than I (am).

She is not as tall as he (is).

They work longer hours than we (do).

AS A SUBJECT COMPLEMENT: A subject complement is a word or word group coming after some form of the verb *to be* and describing or renaming the subject. When the subject complement is a pronoun (usually called a *predicate pronoun*), it must be a subject pronoun.

That is she *[not* her*] in the front row. (She is a predicate pronoun because it follows the linking verb* is *and renames or identifies the subject* That.*)*

The last ones to cross the line were Larry and I *[not* me*]. (I follows the linking verb* were *and, with* Larry, *means the same as the subject* ones. *Therefore, the subject form* I *is needed.)*

Everyone knew that it was they *[not* them*]. (Like the two sentences above, the pronoun following the linking verb identifies the subject and is therefore in the subject form.)*

NOTE: Some exceptions to this rule are allowed. *It is me, It is her,* and *It is them,* for example, are widely used and accepted in informal situations. In formal speaking and writing, however, the preferred forms are *It is I, It is she,* and *It is they.* Follow the advice of your instructor.

AS AN APPOSITIVE IDENTIFYING THE SUBJECT: Subject pronouns should be used when they appear in phrases immediately after the subject or subject complement and mean the same as the subject. Such phrases are called *appositives,* and they can occur in other parts of the sentence as well.

Only two members, Dean and I *[not* me*], voted for an increase in dues. (I, (I, a subject pronoun, is in an appositive phrase renaming the subject,* members.*)*

The exceptions were the two new members, Ron and I *[not* me*]. (I is in an appositive phrase renaming the subject complement,* members.*)*

Tips for Using Subject Pronouns

1. Memorize the subject pronouns: *I, you, he, she, it, who, whoever, we,* and *they.*
2. Remember that only subject pronouns can be subjects of verbs.
3. If a pronoun is part of a compound subject, break the sentence into two parts "My brother and me get along well" is incorrect, as revealed by the following test: "My brother gets along well. I get along well. My brother and *I* get along well."

Exercise 1:

In the following sentences underline every pronoun used as the subject of a verb *and write "A" above it. Underline all pronouns used as a* subject complement *and write "B" above them. Underline all pronouns used as* appositives identifying the subject *and write "C" above them.*

1. Connie has taken more courses in data processing than I.

2. The three people who came to the reunion from the farthest distance— Jack, Bernie, and she—were given prizes by the homecoming committee.

3. If we had worked as hard as they, we would have finished the job by now.

4. It was I who broke the dish.

5. My father taught my brother and me to operate a lathe when we were children.

6. Melissa showed Marti and me the wedding gifts she had received.

7. The dog wagged its tail at Jeff and me, but we were afraid to open the gate and walk into the yard.

8. Many people are surprised when they hear themselves on a tape recording.

9. My old roommate, whom I haven't seen in years, is coming to visit me next week.

10. When the veterinarian handed the puppies to Betsy and me, they began to bark.

The Object Pronouns *(me, you, him, her, it, whom, whomever, us, them)*

As their name suggests, object pronouns are used as objects: *objects of prepositions, direct objects of verbs,* and *indirect objects.*

AS THE OBJECT OF A PREPOSITION   In Chapter 1 you saw that a preposition is followed by a noun or pronoun, called the *object of the preposition*. When the object of the preposition is a pronoun, it must be from the list of object pronouns.

Between you and me *[not* I*], his singing is off-key.*

Her smiling parents stood next to her *at the capping ceremony.*

Solar energy is a possible answer to the energy problems faced by us *[not* we*] Americans.*

When the objects of a preposition are a noun *and* a pronoun, there is a mistaken tendency to use the subject form of the pronoun, as in the sentence below:

(incorrect)   Les offered a piece of his birthday cake to Terry and *I.* (*I* is incorrect because it is a subject pronoun; after a preposition, an object pronoun should be used.)

The best way to correct sentences like this is to break them up into separate sentences. Study the following carefully.

Les offered a piece of his birthday cake to *Terry.*
Les offered a piece of his birthday cake to *me.*
(correct)   Les offered a piece of his birthday cake to *Terry and me.*

AS DIRECT OBJECTS   A direct object is the word that receives the action of the verb. It can follow only an action verb, never a linking verb. When a pronoun is used as a direct object, it must be an object pronoun.

The falling tree missed him *by only a few feet.*

My big brother took me *with him on his first date.*

Please call us *if you get lost.*

Dick married her *before going to boot camp.*

As in the case of prepositions, when both a noun and a pronoun are the direct objects of the same verb, the object form for the pronoun is used. Notice the following:

(incorrect)   Sheila surprised Bob and *I* with her answer.

By breaking up this sentence into two separate sentences, you can determine the correct form:

Sheila surprised *Bob* with her answer.
Sheila surprised *me* with her answer.
(correct)   Sheila surprised *Bob and me* with her answer.

In some sentences a pronoun will be the object of an implied verb. This occurs frequently in comparisons introduced by *than* and *as*. In such cases the object form of the pronoun should be used. (Compare this construction with pronouns used as the subjects of implied verbs, as explained on page 58.) In the following sentences, the implied subjects and verbs are in parentheses.

> *Lorraine knows my brother much better than* (she knows) me.
>
> *The nurse said the shot would hurt her as much as* (it hurt) him.

Using the correct pronoun after *than* and *as* is important, as the following sentences show. What is the difference in meaning between these sentences?

> *My girl friend likes pizza more than* I.
>
> *My girl friend likes pizza more than* me.

AS INDIRECT OBJECTS   An *indirect object* is the person or thing to whom or for whom something is done. The indirect object may be thought of as the recipient of the direct object, and it almost always comes between the action verb and the direct object. When a pronoun is used as an indirect object, the object form of the pronoun should be used.

> *The mail-carrier gave* me *a registered letter.*
>
> *The dealer offered* Alex and her *a discount on the tires.*
>
> *Professor Kirby sent* us *a postcard from England.*

Tips For Using Object Pronouns

---

1. Memorize the object pronouns: *me, you, him, her, it, whom, whomever, us, them.*
2. Use object pronouns when they follow action verbs and prepositions.
3. Never say or write ''between you and *I.*'' The correct form is ''between you and *me.*''

Exercise 2:

In the following sentences underline every object pronoun and write the appropriate letter above it corresponding to its use in the sentence:

      a. *object of a preposition*

      b. *direct object*

      c. *indirect object*

1. The clerk at the hardware store gave George and me some good ideas for refinishing the cabinets.

2. Walt sat behind David and me at the concert last night.

3. The landlord told *B* us that our stereo was too loud.

4. Rich quit *C* his job because it no longer interested him.

5. The clerks will assist *B* you in making your purchase.

6. Between *A* you and *A* me, purple does not look good on Margo.

7. The insurance salesperson explained to *A* us the advantages of term insurance.

8. The tire dealer offered *C* me a discount if I bought a set of four tires.

9. Sharon married *B* him despite the advice of her mother.

10. Because *A* he did not want to disappoint *A* his parents, Joe did not tell *B* them that he had failed algebra.

Exercise 3:

Write the letter corresponding to the correct pronoun.

_B_ 1. A messenger delivered the flowers to Helen and (a. I   b. me).

_A_ 2. Because of the lightning, Rick and (a. he   b. him) left.

_B_ 3. Please leave the door of the garage unlocked for Joyce and (a. I   b. me).

_A_ 4. Mr. Spitzer prepared a special dessert for (a. us   b. we) "weight-watchers."

_B_ 5. Car dealers are offering better deals to (a. us   b. we) buyers.

_B_ 6. If you were (a. I   b. me), what would you do?

_A_ 7. Please keep this a secret between you and (a. I   b. me).

_A_ 8. Jack is as dark as (a. she   b. her) from their afternoon at the beach.

_A_ 9. It's difficult to tell the difference between Linda and (a. her   b. she).

_A_ 10. Everyone except Leo and (a. her   b. she) thought the joke was funny.

_B_ 11. (a. Us   b. We) Americans are better fed than our grandparents.

_A_ 12. Because of the icy roads, Luis will be arriving much later than (a. us   b. we).

A 13. The gasoline expenses will be shared by the Mathers and (a. them b. they).

A 14. The travel agency sent Ken and (a. I b. me) some brochures.

AB 15. Keith helped Dick and (a. I b. me) move into our new apartment.

A 16. Ms. Parks was proud of (a. us b. we) finalists in the contest.

B 17. No one could have been happier than (a. I b. me).

B 18. Delia was happy to do the favor for Miguel and (a. I b. me).

A 19. The woman standing in front of Tom and (a. I b. me) is Louise.

A 20. The Bradleys and (a. us b. we) have lived next door to each other for many years.

The Possessive Pronouns

The possessive pronouns are used to show ownership or possession of one person or thing by another. Most pronouns have two possessive forms:

my, mine, our, ours, his, her, hers, its, their, theirs, your, yours

Use *mine, yours, his, hers, its, ours,* or *theirs* when the possessive pronoun is separated from the noun that it refers to:

The decision was mine.

The problem became theirs.

The car keys that were found were hers.

Use *my, your, his, her, its, our,* or *their* when the possessive pronoun comes immediately before the noun it modifies:

It was my *decision.*

It became their *problem.*

She lost her *car keys.*

The possessive form is usually used immediately before a noun ending in *-ing.* (Such nouns are called *gerunds,* and they are formed by adding *-ing* to verbs: *walking, riding, thinking,* and so on.)

The team objected to his *taking credit for the win.*

Professor Bailey did not like our *chewing gum in class.*

Everyone was glad to hear of your *winning a scholarship.*

The possessive forms of *it*, *who*, and *you* cause problems for many writers. Remember that the apostrophe in *it's*, *who's* and *you're* indicates that these words are contractions, not possessive forms. In Chapter 10 we will look closely at the use of the apostrophe in contractions and possessive nouns. Notice the difference between the following pairs of words:

> *The dark clouds on the horizon suggest that* it's *[it is]* *going to rain tonight.*
>
> *A cardiologist spoke to our physical education class on jogging and* its *effects on the cardiovascular system.*
>
> *He thinks that he knows* who's *[who is]* *responsible for this mess.*
>
> Whose *idea was this, anyway?*
>
> You're *[You are]* *expected to be ready by five o'clock.*
>
> *Have* you *memorized* your *lines for the play?*

Tips for Using Possessive Pronouns

The possessive pronouns do not contain apostrophes.
  It's *means* it is *or* it has.
  Who's *means* Who is *or* Who has.
  You're *means* You are.

Exercise 4:

Write the letter corresponding to the correct word.

_____ 1. Connie laughed at (a. him   b. his) dancing the cha-cha while the band played a polka.

_____ 2. My chewing gum has lost (a. its   b. it's) flavor.

_____ 3. The curator of the zoo described the peacock's diet and (a. its   b. it's) plumage.

_____ 4. Did Alvin give any excuse for (a. him   b. his) being late?

_____ 5. The explorers searching for Noah's ark claim that (a. its   b. it's) located on a mountaintop in Turkey.

_____ 6. Ms. Bowman objected to (a. their   b. them) coughing and sneezing while she listened to the radio.

_____ 7. (a. Whose   b. Who's) the author of *Pride and Prejudice?*

_____ 8. Mr. Murphy sang three verses of ''(a. Its   b. It's) a Long Way to Tipperary.''

_____ 9. (a. Its   b. It's) unlikely that the U.N. will approve the British resolution.

_____ 10. If you eat fatty foods and never exercise, (a. your   b. you're) a likely candidate for high blood pressure.

_____ 11. The gardener fertilized the bush because (a. its   b. it's) leaves were brown.

_____ 12. Nancy Davis was a Hollywood actress (a. whose   b. who's) career was cut short by her marriage to Ronald Reagan.

_____ 13. According to sociobiologists, (a. your   b. you're) intelligence is partially determined by your genetic inheritance.

_____ 14. Clara was disappointed by (a. him   b. his) coming home intoxicated.

_____ 15. Anyone (a. whose   b. who's) suffered from asthma should avoid smog.

The Relative Pronouns _(which, what, who, whose, whom, that, whatever, whoever, whomever)_

Relative pronouns can be used in two ways in a sentence: they can connect one clause with another, and they can act as subjects or objects in their own clauses.

As connecting words:

Famine is one of the major problems that _Africa faces._

He usually accomplishes whatever _he tries to do._

As subjects or objects in their own clauses:

Bob Beamon's record for the long jump, which _has never been surpassed, was set in Mexico City in 1976._

Two pedestrians who _were walking near the curb were hit by flying glass._

A girl that _spoke French helped the couple from Paris._

Who, Which and That: Special Uses

As relative pronouns, _who, which,_ and _that_ each have particular uses.

Use _who_ and _whom_ only for people:

Neil Armstrong was the first man who _set foot on the moon._

She is one of those natural athletes who _can play any sport._

Bing Crosby was a singer whom _everyone admired._

Muhammad Ali is an athlete whom _the whole world recognizes._

Use *which* only for animals and things:

Her dog, which *is a dachshund, sleeps under her bed.*

The proposal which *I have offered will not cost more than the other plans.*

Use *that* for animals, people, and things:

A letter that *does not have sufficient postage will be returned to its sender.*

A desk that *belonged to Thomas Jefferson was sold recently for six thousand dollars.*

Every cat that *does not have a license will be put in the animal pound.*

A stranger that *claimed he was lost seized Joe's wallet and ran.*

PRONOUNS ENDING IN -SELF AND -SELVES

Several pronouns end in *-self* or *-selves:*

myself, yourself, himself, herself, itself, ourselves, yourselves, themselves

As *reflexive pronouns,* these pronouns are used when the action of the sentence is done by the subject to himself or herself:

They helped themselves *to the cookies.*

I tried to bathe myself *despite my broken arm.*

As *intensive pronouns,* these words stress or emphasize another noun or pronoun:

She tuned the engine herself.

You yourself *are to blame.*

The President himself *awarded the medals to the astronauts.*

These pronouns should *not* be used in place of a subject or object pronoun:

(Incorrect)   My wife and *myself* would be happy to accept your invitation.
(Correct)   My wife and *I* would be happy to accept your invitation.
(Incorrect)   On behalf of my family and *myself,* I would like to express our gratitude to all of you.
(Correct)   On behalf of my family and *me,* I would like to express our gratitude to all of you.
(Incorrect)   Kevin helped Ray and *myself* install a new carburetor in my Chevrolet.
(Correct)   Kevin helped Ray and *me* install a new carburetor in my Chevrolet.

Never use forms like *hisself, theirself, theirselves,* or *ourself.* These are nonstandard in both informal and formal speech and writing, and they should always be avoided.

More Tips on Pronouns

---

1. *Who* is the subject form; *whom* is the object form.
2. Do not use pronouns ending in *-self* or *-selves* as subjects or objects.
3. Never use *hisself, theirself, theirselves,* or *ourself.*

4

Review Exercise

On the line preceding each sentence, write the letter corresponding to the correct pronoun.

___A___   1. Wayne bruised (a. himself   b. hisself) severely when he slipped on the wet tile.

___A___   2. The ferry caught (a. its   b. it's) anchor in the cables at the dock.

___B___   3. Some nineteenth-century writers (a. which   b. who) were ignored during their time are now read avidly.

___B___   4. Everyone at the party except Laura and (a. I   b. me) wore jeans.

___A___   5. Bobby Fischer, (a. whose   b. who's) victories over the Russian chess champions established his reputation, is a recluse.

___A___   6. In my absence, I hope that Dory and (a. you   b. yourself) will make yourselves at home.

___B___   7. Ralph's parents do not object to (a. him   b. his) going to Europe next summer.

___B___   8. They are probably as embarrassed about the matter as (a. us   b. we).

___A___   9. The storekeeper suggested that you and (a. he   b. him) submit your requisition by next Friday.

___A___   10. The last ones to leave the lab—Jill and (a. I   b. me)—had to wash the beakers and retorts.

___B___   11. The chairman, (a. which   b. who) had just been appointed, announced his resignation.

___A___   12. I was surprised to learn that Cicely and (a. I   b. myself) had graduated from the same high school.

___A___   13. Many people praise garlic for (a. its   b. it's) alleged curative powers.

___A___   14. When Daryl is released from the hospital, he will be able to take care of (a. himself   b. hisself) without the help of a nurse.

___A___   15. Mr. Pauley explained to (a. us   b. we) interns at the station how a television camera works.

_A_ 16. Because Gil belongs to a health club, he works out more than
(a. I   b. me).

_B_ 17. The people who deserve the credit for the success of the picnic are Patrick
and (a. her   b. she).

_A_ 18. The house was painted by Irwin (a. himself   b. hisself) without any
assistance.

_B_ 19. Rick says that he has found a dentist (a. whose   b. who's) painless.

_B_ 20. While we were playing golf, a bolt of lightning struck a tree near Marshall
and (a. I   b. me).

_A_ 21. When we came to this country as teenagers, my sister and
(a. I   b. myself) were surprised at the freedom young people have.

_B_ 22. What will be the effect of this new regulation on David and
(a. I   b. me)?

_A_ 23. According to the label, this package is (a. yours   b. your's).

_B_ 24. Mary played an etude on the piano for Tony and (a. I   b. me).

_A_ 25. The change in the bylaws was designed to give (a. us   b. we) students
more representation.

SENTENCE COMBINING WITH APPOSITIVES

An appositive (page 58) is a noun or noun phrase that is set beside another noun and identifies or explains it:

> *Fran Tarkenton,* the former quarterback of the Minnesota Vikings, *is now a television sports commentator.*

When two related sentences describe or identify the same subject, one of the sentences can usually be made into an appositive and combined with the other sentence:

1. James Fixx was a well-known author of books and articles about jogging. He died of a heart attack while jogging near his home.

(combined)   James Fixx, a well-known author of books and articles about jogging, died of a heart attack while jogging near his home.

2. Cinco de Mayo is a holiday in Mexico. It celebrates the defeat of the French army on May 5, 1862.

(combined)   Cinco de Mayo, a holiday in Mexico, celebrates the defeat of the French army on May 5, 1862.

3. Doctor Petty has written a book about depression and shyness. They are ailments that affect many young people today.

(combined)   Doctor Petty has written a book about depression and shyness, ailments that affect many young people today.

Notice that the appositives in the above combined sentences are set off by commas. The reason is that they are *nonessential* or *nonrestrictive* appositives (see page 165 for an additional discussion of the use of the comma). When an appositive is *essential* or *restrictive* and therefore necessary for the identification of the subject, no commas are required:

> *The French composer* Saint-Saëns *wrote a beautiful cello concerto.*

By changing one of the sentences in each of the following groups into an appositive, combine the following pairs of sentences.

1. Gilda Radner is a comedienne and movie star. She recently married Gene Wilder, who is an actor, writer, and director.

2. Edgar Cayce issued a number of ''revelations'' on a variety of subjects, including the stock market and the end of the world. He was an American prophet and faith healer.

3. "Solitons" are pulses of energy that run along the length of a molecule. They change the molecule's configuration.

4. Former President Ford is an avid golfer. He has occasionally hit a spectator on the head with an errant golf ball.

5. Rick Davis is the president of our Parent-Teacher Organization. He is a decorated veteran who served in the 101st Airborne Division.

Writing Original Sentences with Appositives

Write ten original sentences with appositives. Underline the appositives; remember to set them off with commas when necessary.

5

**Common Errors in Pronoun
Agreement and Reference**

In the previous chapter we noted that pronouns cause a great deal of uncertainty, even among the most educated speakers and writers. Pronoun agreement and reference is an area of usage that causes particular confusion.

Pronouns should agree with the words they refer to. This means, for example, that if a pronoun refers to a plural antecedent, the pronoun should be plural; if the antecedent is singular, the pronoun should also be singular; and if its antecedent is a pronoun in the third person, the pronoun should also be in the third person. (An *antecedent* is the word or term referred to by the pronoun.)

The rules for pronoun agreement and reference are usually easy to follow. However, there are several situations when (for example) the choice of pronoun is not clear or when the antecedent is not obvious. Such cases can result in confusion or ambiguity on the part of the reader as well as the writer. Because pronoun agreement and reference are necessary if your writing is to be logical and effective, this chapter will examine the situations when they are most critical.

AGREEMENT IN NUMBER

A pronoun must agree with its antecedent *in number.* If the antecedent is singular, the pronoun is singular. If the antecedent is plural, the pronoun is plural. This rule poses no problem in sentences in which the pronoun and its antecedents are close, as in the following examples:

> Mary Laine *wants a car, but* she *wants a Cadillac convertible. (The singular pronoun* she *matches its singular antecedent* Mary Laine.)
>
> Her parents *want a car, but* they *want a Datsun 210. (The plural pronoun* they *matches its plural antecedent* parents.)
>
> Andy *lost* his *tickets to the Michael Jackson concert. (The singular pronoun* his *matches its singular antecedent* Andy.)
>
> The dachshund *ran until* it *became tired. (The singular pronoun* it *matches the singular antecedent* dachshund.)

Problems in pronoun agreement occur when the writer loses sight of the antecedent or confuses it with other nouns in the sentence, as in the following sentence:

(Incorrect) The negotiations committee presented *their* recommendations for wages and benefits to the union members and officers.

This sentence is incorrect because the plural pronoun *their* does not agree with its singular antecedent *committee.* How did the writer make this mistake? He or she may have been thinking of the individuals on the committee or of the recommendations that were submitted, or even of the wages, benefits, members, and officers of the union, and therefore selected *their,* a plural pronoun. But the subject *(committee)* is singular, and therefore any pronoun referring to it must be singular.

(Correct)   The negotiations committee presented *its* recommendations for wages and benefits to the union members and officers.

By following these rules, the pronouns in your sentences will agree with their antecedents in number:

1. In general, use a *singular pronoun* when the antecedent is an *indefinite pronoun.* (For a review of indefinite pronouns, see Chapter 3.) Some indefinite pronouns present exceptions to this rule—they are always plural, or they can be singular or plural depending on the kind of noun they represent.
   a.   The following indefinite pronouns are always *singular:*

   another, anybody, anyone, anything, each, each one, either, every, everybody, everyone, everything, many a, much, neither, nobody, no one, nothing, one, other, somebody, someone, something

   Anyone *planning a trip to Russia should apply for a visa before* he *leaves this country.*

   Each *of the girls told me* her *name.*

   When I returned, everything *was in* its *place.*

   Many a son *wishes* he *had listened to* his *father's advice.*

   Everyone *was asked to contribute as much as* he *could.*

   Everybody *is responsible for making* his *own bed.*

   Neither *of the girls wanted* her *picture taken.*

   You probably noticed the use of masculine pronouns *(he* and *his)* in the first, fifth, and sixth sentences preceding. Many modern writers and readers object to the exclusive use of masculine pronouns with indefinite pronouns such as *anybody, everyone, someone,* and *everybody.* Note carefully the following sentence:

   Everyone took his *seat.*

   This is traditional usage, with *his* used to refer to humanity in general. To avoid the sole use of masculine pronouns, some writers would word the sentence like this:

   Everyone took his or her *seat.*

   Because this form can be awkward, some writers prefer the following method to avoid only masculine pronouns:

   Everyone took their *seats.*

While avoiding the exclusive use of the masculine pronoun, this sentence combines a plural pronoun *(their)* with a singular antecedent *(Everyone)*. Those who prefer this version should be aware that it is not yet accepted in formal written English.

What is the answer to this dilemma? An increasingly popular solution is to reword the sentence, making the subject plural:

The audience *[or* Members *of the audience] took* their *seats.*

b.   The following indefinite pronouns are always *plural:*

both, few, many, others, several

When they are used as antecedents, pronouns referring to them are always *plural:*

Many *of his customers transferred* their *business to another company.*

A few *of the students admitted* they *had not studied.*

Several *of the golfers said* they *wanted to bring their own caddies.*

Both *of the cars had* their *mufflers replaced.*

c.   The following indefinite pronouns can be either singular or plural:

all, any, more, most, none, some

When they are used as antecedents, pronouns referring to them will be either singular or plural, depending on their meaning and the noun they represent:

(plural)	*Most* of the customers wanted onions on *their* hamburgers.
(singular)	*Most* of the tree had been stripped of *its* fruit.
(plural)	*All* of the leaks have been traced to *their* sources.
(singular)	*All* of the water had leaked from *its* container.
(plural)	*Some* of the customers wanted *their* money back.
(singular)	*Some* of the money was returned to *its* hiding place.

Exercise 1:

On the line before each sentence, write the letter indicating the correct pronoun.

_____ 1.   Every player on the girls' basketball team must furnish (a. her   b. their) own uniform and shoes.

_____ 2.   Both statues were repainted in (a. its   b. their) original colors.

_____ 3.   Some members of American Indian tribes do not want anthropologists digging up (a. its   b. their) ancient burial sites.

_____ 4. When answering the telephone, one should speak clearly and slowly so that (a. he   b. they) can be easily understood.

_____ 5. Each of the families attending the picnic was responsible for bringing (a. its   b. their) own food and drinks.

_____ 6. Some of the early settlers in this country passed religious laws as intolerant as those that (a. he   b. they) had previously suffered.

_____ 7. At a recent meeting of divorced fathers in our city, each father brought (a. his   b. their) children.

_____ 8. Anyone buying a used car must get a smog certificate before (a. he   b. they) can purchase new license plates.

_____ 9. Some of the acid rain has been traced to Midwestern manufacturing plants, but some of (a. it   b. them) cannot be explained.

_____ 10. Depending on (a. his   b. their) bone structure, all human beings can be divided into four basic physical types.

2. Antecedents joined by *and* usually take plural pronouns:

Simon and Garfunkel *gave* their *last concert in Central Park.*
Tony and Marie *have decided that* they *will change* their *majors.*

When the antecedents refer to a single person or thing, the pronoun may be singular:

The scientist and author was able to present her *theories in terms that the students could understand.*
The largest tree and oldest living thing on earth, the Sequoiadendron giganteum *is better known by* its *familiar name, the* Giant Sequoia.

When the compound antecedent is preceded by *each* or *every,* a singular pronoun should be used:

Each *jury member and alternate received a letter thanking* him *for* his *participation.*
Every *mother and daughter was assigned to* her *table.*

3. Collective nouns (see Chapter 3) usually take singular pronouns if the group is regarded as a unit:

The couple *was honored for* its *contribution to the church.*
The faculty *was renowned for* its *research and scholarship.*

If the members of the group are acting separately, a plural pronoun should be used:

The couple *disagreed over the amount of money* they *should pay for a new car.*

The faculty *were paid various amounts, depending on* their *education, experience, and publications.*

4. When two or more antecedents are joined by *or* or *nor,* the pronoun should agree with the nearer antecedent:

    Neither Babe Ruth nor *Ted Williams is remembered for* his *fielding ability.*

    Neither the defendant nor *the witnesses changed* their *testimony.*

    Neither the roofers nor *the carpenters finished* their *work on schedule.*

    When the antecedent closer to the pronoun is singular, the result can sometimes be awkward:

    Neither the sopranos nor *the tenor could sing* his *part without looking at* his *music. (Though technically correct, this sentence is confusing.)*

    Such a sentence should be revised:

    Neither the tenor nor *the sopranos could sing* their *parts without looking at their music.*

5. Pronouns that are used as *demonstrative adjectives (this, that, these, those)* must agree in number with the nouns they modify. Do *not* say ''these kind,'' ''these sort,'' ''those kind,'' ''those type,'' and so on. The correct form is ''these kinds,'' ''these sorts,'' ''this kind,'' ''this sort,'' ''that kind,'' ''those kinds,'' and so on.

The following sentences illustrate the use of pronouns as demonstrative adjectives:

(incorrect) These kind of trees are common throughout the South.
  (correct) This kind of tree is common throughout the South. *(Or:* These kinds of trees are common throughout the South.)
(incorrect) These type of ball bearings never need lubrication.
  (correct) This type of ball bearings never needs lubrication. *(Or:* These types of ball bearings never need lubrication.)

TIPS ON PRONOUN AGREEMENT

Pronouns should agree in number with the nouns they stand for.
1. Determine which noun is the real antecedent.
2. Determine whether the antecedent is singular or plural in meaning.
3. Singular pronouns must refer to singular antecedents; plural pronouns must refer to plural antecedents.

Exercise 2:

On the line before each sentence, write the letter corresponding to the correct pronoun.

_____ 1. The family decided to sell (a. its   b. their) individual shares in the company.

_____ 2. The Brazilian team surprised everyone by (a. its   b. their) defeat of the Canadian basketball team.

_____ 3. Each bush and tree was classified according to (a. its   b. their) growing period.

_____ 4. The corporation released (a. its   b. their) statement to the press.

_____ 5. Neither the priest nor the altar boy (a. was   b. were) able to light the candles.

_____ 6. The Leonetti family received (a. its   b. their) passports from the New Orleans office.

_____ 7. (a. These   b. This) kind of math problem requires a knowledge of calculus.

_____ 8. The noted philosopher and poet was reluctant to lecture without (a. her   b. their) notes.

_____ 9. Every bottle of wine and cognac was labeled according to the country (a. it   b. they) came from.

_____ 10. Neither of the daughters had remembered (a. her   b. their) mother's birthday.

AGREEMENT IN PERSON

You have seen that pronouns agree in number with their antecedents. If the agreement breaks down, the reader is distracted and confused. Agreement in *person* is equally important. *Person* refers to the difference between the person speaking (first person), the person spoken to (second person), and the person or thing spoken about (third person).

First person pronouns:	I, me, my, mine, we, us, ours, our
Second person pronouns:	you, your, yours
Third person pronouns:	he, him, his, she, her, hers, it, its, they, them, theirs

When you make a mistaken shift in person, you have shown that you have lost your way in your own sentence—that you have forgotten what you were writing about. Here are some examples of confusing shifts in person:

(shift)   Swimmers in the ocean should be very careful because *you* can get caught in riptides. (This sentence shifts from third person "Swimmers" to second person "you.")

(revised)   Swimmers in the ocean should be very careful because *they* can get caught in riptides.

(shift)   When you fly to St. Louis, *passengers* can see the arch on the bank of the Mississippi River from miles away. (This sentence shifts from second person "you" to third person "passengers.")

(revised)   When you fly to St. Louis, *you* can see the arch on the bank of the Mississippi River from miles away.

(shift)   When *I* entered the room, *you* could smell the fresh paint.

(revised)   When *I* entered the room, *I* could smell the fresh paint.

The best way to avoid such shifts is to decide in advance whom you are talking about—and stick with that point of view.

Exercise 3:

Correct any errors involving needless shift of person in the following sentences. If a sentence is correct, mark it "C."

1. I have found that if I want something done right, you should do it yourself.

2. At many hotels in Europe, guests are required to turn in your passports when checking in.

3. Persons driving for the first time in England should remember that you have to drive on the left side of the road.

4. If a student works hard in Professor Stewart's class, you can expect to get a good grade.

5. Everyone should keep a careful record of income and expenses in case you are audited by the Internal Revenue Service.

6. When you read your first Russian novel, it is difficult for the reader to keep in mind the names of all the characters.

7. If you want to become a good chess player, you should read articles about the game and enter tournaments.

8. When a person wakes up with a hangover after six martinis, you should not blame the olives.

9. Whenever I see my Uncle Bert, I am reminded of Milton Berle.

10. If you have ever heard her voice, you will never forget it.

PRONOUN REFERENCE

Pronouns have no identity of their own. They depend on other words—their antecedents—for their meaning. If their relationship to their antecedents is unclear, their meaning or identity will be confusing. For this reason, you should make certain that every pronoun in your writing (except for indefinite pronouns like *anyone* and *somebody,* and idioms like "*It* is two o'clock") refers specifically to something previously named—its antecedent. In doing so, you will avoid the two most common kinds of problems in pronoun reference: *vagueness* because the writer did not furnish a specific antecedent, and *ambiguity* because the writer supplied too many antecedents.

Here is an example of each kind of error:

(vague)   Several minor political parties nominate presidential candidates every four years. This is one of the characteristics of the American political system. (*What* is one of the characteristics of the American political system?)

(ambiguous)   Gore Vidal recently wrote a biography of Abraham Lincoln which demonstrates his knowledge and sensitivity. (*Who* demonstrates his knowledge and sensitivity: Gore Vidal or Abraham Lincoln?)

By following these rules, you can make clear the relationship between pronouns and their antecedents:

1.   The antecedent of a pronoun should be specific rather than implied. Avoid using *that, this, which,* and *it* to refer to implied ideas unless the reference is unmistakably clear.

(vague)   Kent was so impressed by the lecture given by the astronomer that he decided to major in it. (Major in what? *It* has no antecedent in this sentence.)

(revision)   Kent was so impressed by the lecture given by the astronomer that he decided to major in astronomy.

(vague)   Brad consumes huge quantities of potatoes, spaghetti, and ice cream every day, and it is beginning to be noticeable. (What is beginning to be noticeable?)

(revision)   Brad consumes huge quantities of potatoes, spaghetti, and ice cream every day, and the increase in his weight is beginning to be noticeable.

(vague)	Helen enjoys singing with music groups at school, and she would like to be a professional one someday. (A professional what?)
(revision)	Helen enjoys singing with music groups at school, and she would like to be a professional singer someday.

Such vague sentences are corrected by supplying the missing antecedent. Some sentences, however, are confusing because they have more than one possible antecedent, and the result is ambiguity.

2.   To avoid ambiguity or confusion, place pronouns as close as possible to their antecedents. Revise sentences in which there are two possible antecedents for a pronoun.

(confusing)	Connie's new car has leather seats, a sunroof, a digital dash with graphic read-outs, a vocal warning system, power windows, and an eight-speaker stereo. It is power driven. (What does *It* refer to? What is power driven?)
(revision)	Connie's new car has leather seats, a sunroof which is power driven, a digital dash with graphic read-outs, a vocal warning system, power windows, and an eight-speaker stereo.
(confusing)	Spanish cooking and Mexican cooking should not be confused; it is not as spicy. (What is not as spicy?)
(revision)	Spanish cooking is not as spicy as Mexican cooking.
(confusing)	The dish has been in our family for one hundred years that you dropped.
(revision)	The dish that you dropped has been in our family for one hundred years.

Tips on Pronoun Reference

---

1. Don't shift pronouns unnecessarily from one person to another.
2. Learn the pronouns for first, second, and third person.
3. Make sure that every *that, this, which,* and *it* in your sentences has an antecedent.
4. Place pronouns as close as possible to their antecedents.

Exercise 4:

Rewrite the following sentences to make clear the vague or ambiguous pronoun references. You may add, omit, or change words as necessary.

1. Although Todd has never been there, he prefers French wines.

2. Many advertising agencies have psychologists on their staffs because it is important in selling a product.

3. Pablo Casals was a great cellist who claimed that he had practiced it every day for almost eighty years.

4. Interest rates continue to rise and the average price of a home goes up every month. This makes it almost impossible for a young couple to buy a house.

5. As Maureen and Jennifer talked, her voice began to tremble.

6. Mel took ice-skating lessons but still isn't able to do it very well.

7. After having her own room all of her life, Muriel has moved into a dormitory room which has created several problems.

8. Ray's secret ambition is to be a bullfighter, but he has never gone to one.

9. In high school they take roll in every class every day.

10. Warren is a very shy boy, but he keeps it hidden.

5

Review Exercise

A. *Write the letter of the correct response.*

___A___ 1. The terms ''singular'' and ''plural'' refer to:

    a. number b. part of speech c. tense d. all of the above

___C___ 2. Pronouns should agree with the _____ they refer to.

    a. adjective b. adverb c. antecedent d. none of the above

___B___ 3. *Another, anything, either, everything, nobody,* and *someone* are examples of:

    a. singular verbs   c. common nouns

    b. indefinite pronouns   d. conjunctions

___A___ 4. What do the following pronouns have in common: *all, any, more, most, none, some?*

    a. they can be either singular or plural   c. they are always plural

    b. they are always singular   d. none of the above

___B___ 5. What do the following pronouns have in common: *both, few, many, several?*

    a. they are always singular   c. they can be either singular or plural

    b. they are always plural   d. none of the above

___D___ 6. When *each one, many a, much,* and *something* are used as antecedents, pronouns referring to them are always:

    a. capitalized b. in the past tense c. in the first person d. singular

___C___ 7. Which of the following is incorrect:

    a. this kind b. that kind c. these kind d. those kinds

___D___ 8. Pronouns should always be:

    a. at the beginning of a sentence   c. shifted from one person to another

    b. capitalized   d. as close as possible to their antecedents

___A___ 9. Which of the rules below has been violated in this sentence: ''When you consider how much money the government collects in taxes, it makes a person wonder where it all goes.''

    a. agreement in person   c. subject-verb agreement

    b. agreement in gender   d. agreement in principle

_____C_____ 10. Which of the following pronouns is not in the third person:

a. he   b. its   c. our   d. their

B. *Write the letter of the correct pronoun.*

_____A_____ 11. No one who had thought about it would have given (a. his   b. their) approval to the project.

_____A_____ 12. (a. That   b. Those) kind of grass is often used on golf courses.

_____B_____ 13. Neither the hammer nor the nails were in (a. its   b. their) proper places in the toolshed.

_____B_____ 14. Both Ann and Martha have begun (a. her   b. their) experiments.

_____A_____ 15. Neither Bill nor Arnold arrived at (a. his   b. their) destination on time.

_____A_____ 16. Someone neglected to pick up (a. his   b. their) change from the counter.

_____A_____ 17. Every student planning to attend summer school was asked to turn in (a. his   b. their) application by next Monday.

_____A_____ 18. Doctors urge anyone with (a. that   b. those) kind of allergy to remain indoors during the smog alert.

_____A_____ 19. A motorcyclist should always look ahead at least two cars so that (a. he   b. they) can be prepared for a sudden stop.

_____A_____ 20. The judge complimented the jury for (a. its   b. their) verdict.

_____A_____ 21. Anyone who would invest in such an outrageous scheme should have (a. his   b. their) head examined.

_____A_____ 22. The banker claimed that anyone with an average income should invest at least one-fourth of (a. his   b. your) savings in real estate.

_____A_____ 23. The orchestra was known for (a. its   b. their) recordings of Viennese waltzes.

_____A_____ 24. Many a prospector looked for gold in Alaska or California before (a. he   b. they) finally gave up in despair.

_____B_____ 25. Many of the jobs at the factory were not filled because (a. it   b. they) required experience and an expensive set of tools.

SENTENCE COMBINING WITH PARTICIPLES

Participles are forms of the verb that work as adjectives. The *present* participle is the *-ing* form when it is used as an adjective: his *swimming* pool, a *throbbing* headache, her *smiling* face. The *past* participle is the *-d, -ed, -t,* or *-n* form of the verb when it is used as an adjective: the *painted* house, a *proven* fact, a *kept* promise, the *stated* argument.

Two sentences can often be combined by changing one of them into a participial phrase:

1. Steve whistled as he walked up to his girl friend's house. He was trying to appear nonchalant.
(combined)   Trying to appear nonchalant, Steve whistled as he walked up to his girl friend's house. *(present participle)*
2. The Vietnam War Memorial in Washington attracts thousands of visitors every week. It is dedicated to the American soldiers who were killed in Vietnam.
(combined)   The Vietnam War Memorial in Washington, dedicated to the American soldiers killed in Vietnam, attracts thousands of visitors every week. (Notice that two past participles are used in this sentence: *dedicated* and *killed.*)
3. The President spotted a band of photographers and reporters. He waved to them and entered his helicopter.
(combined)   Spotting a band of photographers and reporters, the President waved to them and entered his helicopter. *(present participle)*

Using present and past participles, combine the following pairs of sentences.

1. Last week a car bomb wrecked an American outpost in Lebanon. This time it killed at least twelve people.

2. The attorney argued that there is a bond between a lawyer and his client. He argued that the bond is protected by the Constitution.

3. The project started with an original staff of fifteen people in 1978. Now the project employs a total of 107 staff members.

4. Jeff studied the poetry of the Romatic poets. He realized that he would never be a poet.

5. The bull was exhausted, weakened, and taunted. Finally, it collapsed to the floor of the arena.

Writing Original Sentences with Present and Past Participles

Write ten original sentences, using present and past participles. Underline present participles once, and past participles twice.

6

Common Errors Involving Verbs

One reason why many mistakes are made in verb usage is that every sentence contains at least one verb, and consequently there are more chances to go wrong. Furthermore, the verbs most often used in the English language are irregular, which means that they change in a variety of ways that makes any kind of generalization about them impossible. This also means that they must be memorized. To make matters even worse, verbs change their forms and appearance more often than any other part of speech, offering us a series of choices and snares that force us to pick our way through them carefully and deliberately.

Is the case hopeless, then? Is it impossible to learn to use verbs correctly and confidently? Not at all; despite the difficulties mentioned above, problems with verbs fall into a few manageable categories. A common problem, for instance, is not knowing the correct form of the verb in order to express when a particular action is taking place. Another difficulty is not knowing the correct form of an irregular verb. This chapter will present solutions to these and other common problems that many writers and speakers have in using verbs.

Before we begin, however, look at the following sentences to see whether you use the correct verb form. Each sentence contains a verb that is often used incorrectly. The incorrect verb is in brackets.

> *After much teasing and pleading, Tim's girl friend* dragged *[not ''drug'']* *the secret out of him.*
>
> *Although I* saw *[not ''seen'']* *the movie a year ago, I can still remember the opening scene in detail.*
>
> *Marcia had* gone *[not ''went'']* *to class three weeks before she realized she was in the wrong room.*
>
> *Roberta's heart* sank *[not ''sunk'']* *when the letter carrier did not bring any mail.*
>
> *Laine* sneaked *[not ''snuck'']* *out of church just as the sermon began.*

If you discovered that you have been using any of these verbs incorrectly, this chapter will give you some practical tips for their correct use. We will begin by examining the principal parts of regular and irregular verbs, moving next to the most common problems connected with the use of verbs, including shifts in tense and troublesome pairs like *lie* and *lay,* and *sit* and *set.*

REGULAR VERBS

All verbs have four principal parts: the *present,* the *past,* the *past participle,* and the *present participle.* By learning these four parts you can build all of the verb tenses. Incidentally, the word *tense* comes from a Latin word meaning *time.* When we talk about the *tense* of a verb, therefore, we mean the *time* expressed by a verb: the *present* tense (or time), the *past* tense, and the *future* tense.

Regular verbs form the *past* and *past participle* by adding *-ed* or *-d* to their present-tense forms. The past participle is the form used with the helping verbs *have, has,* or *had* or with a form of *be (am, is, are, was, were).* The *present participle* is formed by adding *-ing* to the present form, and it is used with *am, is, are, was,* or *were* to form the *progressive tenses* (I am studying, I was studying, I have been studying, and so on).

Here are the four principal parts of some common regular verbs.

Present	Past	Past Participle	Present Participle
talk	talked	talked	talking
use	used	used	using
watch	watched	watched	watching
love	loved	loved	loving
help	helped	helped	helping

Notice that the past tense form *(talked, used, watched,* and so on) and the past participle are identical and are formed by adding *-ed* to the present tense form. Notice, too, that the past participle form is used with helping verbs: I *have* talked, I *had* talked, she *has* talked; I *was* helped, we *were* helped, they *had been* helped, and so on.

IRREGULAR VERBS

Irregular verbs are irregular in the way their past tense and past participle forms are made. Instead of adding *-ed* or *-d,* they change in a variety of ways that make any kind of generalization impossible. This means that you will have to memorize the past tense and past participle forms of the irregular verbs. Fortunately, irregular verbs form their present participles in the same way as regular verbs: by adding *-ing* to the present form.

To understand why it is difficult to make any generalization about irregular verbs, let us examine the verbs *sing* and *bring.* From our familiarity with the English language we know that *sing* is present tense ("I *sing* in church every Sunday"), *sang* is past tense ("I *sang* last Sunday"), and *sung* is the past participle ("I have *sung* every Sunday this month"). Imagine the confusion of someone learning English who, having mastered *sing,* applies the same changes by analogy to the verb *bring.* He logically concludes that the past tense of *bring* is *brang* ("I *brang* my lunch yesterday") and that the past participle is *brung* ("I have *brung* my lunch"). To native speakers of English these forms are humorous; to others who have not mastered the inconsistencies of our verbs, there is nothing within the verb *bring* to suggest that the past tense and past participle are *brought* ("I *brought* my lunch yesterday" and "I *have brought* my lunch").

The English language contains over two hundred irregular verbs, and they are the verbs most often used. Consult your dictionary if you are not sure

© 1986 Scott, Foresman and Company

about the past tense and past participle forms of irregular verbs. Don't trust your ear; what "sounds right" may only be the result of having repeatedly heard, said, and written the incorrect form. The "piano" you have been playing all these years may be out of tune.

Below is a list of some of the most common irregular verbs, as well as a few regular verbs that often present problems. Practice their correct forms by putting "I" in front of the present and past tense forms, "I have" in front of the past participle form, and "I am" in front of the present participle form: "I *begin. I began. I have begun. I am beginning.*" Practice saying them correctly until they sound correct and natural.

Present	Past Tense	Past Participle	Present Participle
arise	arose	arisen	arising
awake	awoke (or awaked)	awaked, awoken	awaking
bear	bore	born (pertaining to birthdate)	bearing
		borne (carried)	
begin	began	begun	beginning
blow	blew	blown	blowing
break	broke	broken	breaking
bring	brought	brought	bringing
burst	burst	burst	bursting
catch	caught	caught	catching
choose	chose	chosen	choosing
come	came	come	coming
dig	dug	dug	digging
dive	dived, dove	dived	diving
do	did	done	doing
drag	dragged	dragged	dragging
draw	drew	drawn	drawing
drink	drank	drunk	drinking
drive	drove	driven	driving
drown	drowned	drowned	drowning
eat	ate	eaten	eating
fly	flew	flown	flying
freeze	froze	frozen	freezing
give	gave	given	giving
go	went	gone	going

Present	Past Tense	Past Participle	Present Participle
grow	grew	grown	growing
hang	hung	hung	hanging
hang (executed)	hanged	hanged	hanging
hide	hid	hidden	hiding
know	knew	known	knowing
lay	laid	laid	laying
lead	led	led	leading
leave	left	left	leaving
lie	lay	lain	lying
light	lighted, lit	lighted, lit	lighting
ride	rode	ridden	riding
ring	rang	rung	ringing
rise	rose	risen	rising
run	ran	run	running
see	saw	seen	seeing
set	set	set	setting
shake	shook	shaken	shaking
shine (glow)	shone	shone	shining
shine (polish)	shined	shined	shining
shrink	shrank, shrunk	shrunk, shrunken	shrinking
sing	sang	sung	singing
sink	sank	sunk	sinking
sit	sat	sat	sitting
sleep	slept	slept	sleeping
sneak	sneaked	sneaked	sneaking
speed	sped	sped	speeding
spring	sprang	sprung	springing
swim	swam	swum	swimming
swing	swung	swung	swinging
take	took	taken	taking
tear	torn	torn	tearing
throw	threw	thrown	throwing
wake	woke, waked	waked, woken	waking

Present	Past Tense	Past Participle	Present Participle
wear	wore	worn	wearing
write	wrote	written	writing

Suggestions for Using Irregular Verbs

1. Resist the temptation to add *-ed* to an irregular verb: do not write or say catch*ed*, burst*ed*, know*ed*, and so on.

2. Be sure that you use the correct form after forms of the helping verbs *have* and *be.*

   Have, has, and *had* are used before the *past participle* (the forms in the third column above):

She has done *field studies in Africa.*

We had spoken *to Martin before he left.*

They have sold *their home and moved to Cincinnati.*

   Am, are, is, was, were, has been, and other forms of *be* are used with the past participle forms to form all passive voice verbs:

The contract was broken *as a result of their disagreement.*

Two bottles of wine were drunk *with the meal.*

Shirley's Fiat had been driven *30,000 miles before it* was sold.

   Forms of *be* are also used before the *present participle* (the forms in the fourth column above) to form the progressive tenses:

Wind surfing is becoming *popular on the East Coast.*

Marty has been awaking *at dawn every day.*

Two dogs were barking *all night in my neighbor's yard.*

Tips on Forming the Past Tense, Past Participle, and Present Participle Forms

1. To form the past tense and past participle forms of a regular verb, add *-ed* or *-d* to the present tense. To form the present participle, add *-ing* to the present tense.
2. Irregular verbs change their spelling and therefore have to be memorized. Study the list on pages 91-93 for the correct past tense and past participle forms of irregular verbs.

Exercise 1:

Fill in the blank in each sentence with the past tense *form of the verb in parentheses.*

_____ 1. The water pipes under our house _____ last winter because of the freezing temperatures. *(burst)*

_____ 2. Mrs. Crowder _____ two sets of twins that no one could tell apart. *(bear)*

_____ 3. Jack _____ the buttons on his uniform until they glistened. *(shine)*

_____ 4. The swallows _____ to Capistrano on schedule last spring. *(fly)*

_____ 5. Vigilantes _____ the cattle rustler before the sheriff could save him. *(hang)*

_____ 6. Tarzan _____ by a vine across the river to surprise Jane. *(swing)*

_____ 7. Young boys _____ off the cliffs looking for coins the tourists had thrown. *(dive)*

_____ 8. The rescue team _____ to the raft containing the three children. *(swim)*

_____ 9. The governor _____ on the float in the annual Homecoming Parade. *(ride)*

_____ 10. Because the team was winning the pennant, it _____ over four million fans during the season. *(draw)*

Exercise 2:

Fill in the blank in each sentence with the past participle *form of the verb in parentheses.*

1. The new year had scarcely _____ when Henry broke all of his resolutions. *(begin)*

2. An unexpected gale had _____ over the wall guarding the estate. *(blow)*

3. The President stated that the Russians had _____ the terms of the treaty. *(break)*

4. Although several bass were _____, some of them were too small to keep. *(catch)*

5. After Silas had brought in the cows and _____ his chores, he studied the Bible. *(do)*

6. Several large bags of sand were _____ across the beach and stacked into a pile as a barricade against the water. *(drag)*

7. Because of the hot weather, a record number of bottles of beer were _____ at the baseball game. *(drink)*

8. According to eyewitnesses, the car was _____ at speeds in excess of one hundred miles an hour. *(drive)*

9. Claiming that he had already _____, Leo did not join us for dinner. *(eat)*

10. Because of the new law, prices have been _____ at their current level. *(freeze)*

USING THE CORRECT TENSE

You have noticed in your study of verbs that they can show different tenses or times by the ending *-ed* or *-d,* by a change in spelling, and by the helping verbs that go with them. The forms of the verb change according to the time expressed—when the action or state of being occurs. Each tense has a specific purpose, and careful speakers and writers select the appropriate tense according to that purpose.

Here is a list of the six common tenses in English and their uses.

Present	*I wait (am waiting)*
Past	*I waited (was waiting)*
Future	*I will* wait (will be waiting)*
Present Perfect	*I have waited (have been waiting)*
Past Perfect	*I had waited (had been waiting)*
Future Perfect	*I will* have waited (will have been waiting)*

The **present tense** is used in the following situations:

a.   To express a condition or action that exists or is going on now.

The soup is *hot.*
Our friends are waiting *for us.*

b.   To express an action that is habitual.

Harold visits *his family every weekend.*
The baby cries *whenever it sees the dog.*

c.   To express a truth or idea that is always true.

Familiarity breeds *contempt.*
Jefferson City is *the capital of Missouri.*

---

*Shall is often substituted for *will* in the future and future perfect tenses.

The **past tense** expresses an action or condition completed in the past.

> *The Japanese* bombed *Pearl Harbor on December 7, 1941.*
> *Hal* moved *to Santa Fe last month.*

The **future tense** expresses an action that will take place in the future.

> *Susan* will graduate *in two years.*
> *My grandmother* will be *eighty next week.*

The **present perfect tense** expresses an action or condition that started in the past and has been completed at some indefinite time or is still going on.

> *My French instructor* has studied *at the Sorbonne in Paris.*
> *Mr. and Mrs. Cruz* have lived *in San Antonio for many years.*

The **past perfect tense** expresses an action that was completed before another action in the past occurred.

> *Jackie found the wallet that she* had misplaced.
> *Rick remembered the man who* had spoken *to him earlier.*

The **future perfect tense** indicates an action that will be complete before a particular time in the future.

> *His parents* will have been married *fifty years next Thanksgiving.*
> *She* will have called *me by the time you arrive next week.*

A Few Suggestions for Using the Correct Tense

1. Don't use the past tense of a verb when it should be in the present tense.

> *Margie took a course in anthropology last year. She said that it* was *an interesting subject that studied cultures and societies throughout the world.* [**Incorrect.** *"Was" and "studied" imply that anthroplogy no longer is interesting and does not study other societies and cultures. The correct verbs are "is" and "studies."*]

2. Use the present infinitive (*to write, to invent, to leap,* and so on) unless the action referred to was completed before the time expressed in the governing verb.

> *Helen and her husband planned to stay [not* to have stayed] *in Miami for two weeks.*
> *I am fortunate to have had [not* to have] *his advice when I was young.*

3. When a narrative in the past tense is interrupted by a reference to a preceding event, use the past perfect tense.

The doctor told the anxious parents that their son had responded *favorably to the treatment.*

The witness admitted that he had lied *about the events of the previous night.*

A Few Reminders about Tenses

1. Use the past tense only if the action referred to took place at a specific time in the past.
2. Use the past perfect tense ("had" plus the past participle) only when you want to place a completed action *before* another action in the past.

Exercise 3:

On the line, identify the tense of the italicized verb by writing past, present, future, present perfect, past perfect, *or* future perfect.

_____ 1. My grandfather often *speaks* of the Great Depression of the 1930s.

_____ 2. Joseph's parents *had never met* before they were engaged because of the religious customs of their country.

_____ 3. Videotape recorders *have become* popular with athletes who want to evaluate their performances.

_____ 4. Ruth uses basil, rosemary, and other herbs when she *makes* soup.

_____ 5. I *will have finished* my report by the time you come home.

_____ 6. The biggest bank in our city *has declared* bankruptcy.

_____ 7. Thomas Jefferson and John Adams *died* on the same day.

_____ 8. The dog *began* to bark when the cat entered the yard.

_____ 9. Although I did not want to admit it, I knew that I *had been* wrong.

_____ 10. If you *had gone* to the doctor, your cold would be better now.

Exercise 4:

On the line preceding each sentence, write the verb shown in parentheses in the tense indicated.

_____ 1. The Northwest Passage *(be—present perfect)* the subject of several historical novels.

_____ 2. Ted jumped from his seat when the balloon *(burst—past tense)*.

_____ 3. Walter *(break—past)* his arm in two places when he fell.

_____ 4. Every time my neighbor *(see—present tense)* a package delivered to my home, he asks me what it is.

_____ 5. Although the Senator *(give—past tense)* no reason for his decision, he announced that he would not run again.

_____ 6. The tourists held their purses and wallets firmly because their guide *(tell—past perfect)* them the area was dangerous.

_____ 7. Gail complained that the horse the rancher *(give—past perfect)* her was too temperamental to ride.

_____ 8. It was not until the waiter *(bring—past tense)* my steak tartar that I realized it was raw hamburger.

_____ 9. Chris took tap-dance lessons when he *(be—past tense)* a child, but he has forgotten most of what he learned.

_____ 10. Reggie *(buy—past tense)* a smoke alarm that is defective.

Shifts in Tense

Having learned the uses of the six common tenses, you should use them consistently, avoiding unnecessary shifts from one tense to another. If, for example, you begin an essay using the past tense to describe events in the past, do not suddenly leap to the present tense to describe those same events. Similarly, don't abruptly shift to the past tense if you are narrating an incident in the present tense. This does not mean that you can't use more than one tense in a piece of writing. It does mean, however, that you must use the same tense when referring to the same period of time.

In the paragraph below, the writer uses past tense verbs to describe events that occurred in the past, and then shifts correctly to the present tense to describe events occurring in the present.

> *I learned to respect fine craftsmen when I was a young boy helping my father build the house that I lived in until I married. My father had an exact, precise air about him that could make sloppy people like me somewhat nervous. When he laid out the dimensions of the house or the opening of*

a door he did it with an exactness and precision that would not allow for the careless kind of measurements that I would settle for. When he measured a board and told me to cut it, I knew that it would have to be cut in an unwavering line and that it would fit exactly in the place assigned to it. Doors that he installed still fit tightly, drawers slide snugly, and joints in cabinets and mortices can scarcely be detected. Today, when I measure a piece of new screenwire to replace the old or a fence to put around the rose bushes, I can still hear the efficient clicking of his six-foot rule as he checks my calculations.

This passage is correct in its use of tenses. The events of the past are recalled by the author and narrated in the past tense ("I learned," "My father had," "he laid out," and so on). When he shifts to the present, he changes his tense accordingly ("Today, when I measure," "I can still hear," and so on). The paragraph below, on the other hand, is confusing because of its inconsistent use of tenses, shifting from the past to the present tense to refer to the same time.

Carl Lewis is one of the world's greatest athletes. As a sprinter and holder of several records he ran effortlessly in the 100, 200, and relays. This is because he approaches running as a science and was interested in the mechanics of the sport. As a long jumper, he hoped to break the record set by Bob Beamon in the 1968 Olympics. Lewis believes that he will eventually equal Beamon's jump. Lewis is regarded by most knowledgeable critics as the best-conditioned all-around athlete in Olympic history. He was admired by the public for his dedication to his sport and for the excitement he brought to track whenever he enters a race.

You probably noticed that the first sentence is in the present tense ("Carl Lewis *is* one of . . ."), signaling the reader that the paragraph will be related in the present tense. Because Carl Lewis is still running, and because the opening sentence is in the present tense, we are not prepared for the second sentence, which abruptly shifts to the past tense ("he *ran* effortlessly"). The third sentence returns to the present tense ("he *approaches*"), and additional changes in the use of tenses continue to add confusion in the rest of the paragraph. The writer of this paragraph could not decide (or perhaps forgot) when the events he was writing about took place. To avoid such confusion, keep in mind the tense forms you are using.

Exercise 5:

Some of the following sentences contain confusing tense shifts. Rewrite them so that the tenses are consistent. If a sentence is correct, mark it "C."

1. Our dog barks angrily when he became frightened.

2. My economics professor said that he enjoyed teaching because it gives him an opportunity to influence the minds of young people.

3. In this afternoon's soap opera, Marcia takes Peter to the hospital when he broke his arm.

4. Frank could not remember where he places his glasses when he went to bed.

5. After washing the car, Hal took a nap and then watches the game on television.

6. Ever since Bert was promoted to department manager, he is unfriendly to us.

7. After I called Gene's home all afternoon with no success, I realize that he is on vacation.

8. Phyllis slept for three hours this afternoon and would have slept even longer if we had not awakened her.

9. The President's announcement that he would select a teacher as a member of the next space flight is greeted with skepticism by many educators.

10. During the opening ceremonies before the game, a dog ran out on the field and bit the umpire.

TWO PAIRS OF IRREGULAR VERBS: *LIE* AND *LAY*; *SIT* AND *SET*

Four irregular verbs cause more trouble than most of the others: *lie* and *lay*, and *sit* and *set.* Unwary speakers and writers can easily confuse them, but careful speakers and writers observe their differences.

Lie and Lay

''To lie'' means ''to remain in position or be at rest'' (We are ignoring the other meaning—''to tell a falsehood''; when *lie* carries this meaning, it is a regular verb.) *Lie* never takes an object—that is, you never *lie* anything down. *Lie* is usually followed by a word or phrase that tells where (*lie* down, *lie* on the grass, and so on).

The principal parts of *lie* are *lie* (the present tense form), *lay* (the past tense), and *lain* (the past participle). The present participle is *lying.* Because our ear tells us that a ''d'' sound is usually the sign of the past tense, we are tempted to say or write *laid* for the past tense, instead of the correct form *lay.*

Present: *Every Sunday afternoon after lunch I* lie *down to take a nap.*
    Past: *Last Sunday I* lay *[not* laid*] down and slept for two hours.*
Present
Perfect: *The dishes have* lain *[not* laid*] in the sink all day.*

The present participle *lying* is used with helping verbs; it should not be confused with *laying*.

The dog has been lying *[not* laying*] on the front porch this afternoon.*

Your keys are lying *[not* laying*] on the bookcase.*

"To lay" means to place or put something somewhere, and it is a *transitive verb*—that is, it requires an object to complete its meaning: lay the *package* down, lay your *head* down, and so on. The principal parts of *lay* are *lay* (present tense), *laid* (past tense), *laid* (past participle), and *laying* (present participle).

Present: *Please* lay *the letter on my desk.*
   Past: *Paul* laid *his head on the table and wept.*
Present
 Perfect: *We* have laid *over six hundred bricks in the new driveway.*

The present participle *laying* is used with helping verbs; it is followed by an object.

We were laying *bricks in uneven lines and had to remove them.*

The campers were laying *dried branches on the campfire.*

The most effective way of mastering *lie* and *lay* is to memorize their forms: *lie, lay, lain, lying; lay, laid, laid, laying.*

Sit and Set

"To sit," meaning "to occupy a seat," is an *intransitive* verb—it never takes an object. This means that you never "sit" anything down, for example. The principal parts are *sit* (the present tense), *sat* (the past tense), and *sat* (the past participle). The present participle is *sitting*. Study the following sentences carefully:

We sit *in the front row of history class this semester.* (present tense)

Last semester we sat *in the back row.* (past tense)

Grace has sat *next to us in Spanish class all year.* (past participle)

Have you been sitting *here long?* (present participle)

"To set" resembles "to lay" in meaning. "To set" means "to put in place," and, like *lay,* it is a *transitive* verb and is followed by another word (a direct object) to complete its meaning.* Its principal parts remain the same in

---

*In a few idioms such as "The hen *sets* on her nest" and "The sun is *setting*," *set* does not require a direct object. In all other cases, however, it is followed by a direct object.

all forms: *set* (present tense), *set* (past tense), and *set* (past particple). The present participle is *setting.* Study the following sentences carefully.

> *Please* set *the thermostat for sixty-eight degrees.* (present tense)
>
> *Last night I* set *the table for four people, but eight showed up.* (past tense)
>
> *I have* set *the sails for a northeastern course.* (past participle)
>
> Setting *his books on the library table, John put his head down and dozed off.* (present participle)

As in the case of *lie* and *lay*, the most effective way of mastering *sit* and *set* is to memorize their forms: *sit, sat, sat, sitting; set, set, set, setting.*

Tips for Using "Lie and Lay" and "Sit and Set"

1. "To lie" means "to be at rest"; you don't *lie* anything down. The forms are *lie, lay, lain,* and *lying.*
2. "To lay" means "to place or put somewhere"; an object must always follow this verb. The forms are *lay, laid, laid,* and *laying.*
3. "To sit" means "to occupy a seat"; you don't *sit* anything down. The forms are *sit, sat, sat,* and *sitting.*
4. "To set" means "to put in place," and except for idioms like "The hen sets" and "The sun sets," it is always followed by an object. The forms do not change in the present and past tenses or the past participle: *set, set,* and *set.* The present participle is *setting.*

Exercise 6:

A. Use the correct form of "lie" and "lay" in the following sentences.

1. Yesterday I _____ in the sun too long and became sunburned.

2. Last summer Max got a job _____ carpeting in a nearby town.

3. Mrs. Parker's newspaper has _____ on her front lawn for three days.

4. Are these your slippers _____ in the middle of the floor, Harry?

5. Please _____ your books and packages down on the sofa.

6. The foundation for our garage will be _____ next week.

7. Gus is content to _____ in the backyard and drink beer all afternoon.

8. Arthur _____ his towel in the sun to dry.

9. My idea of relaxation is to _____ in a Jacuzzi while drinking a glass of hot tea.

10. As I _____ on the doctor's examining table, I could hear the screams of other patients in nearby rooms.

11. I did not realize that I had _____ my hat on a freshly painted table.

12. Sonia has _____ in bed all week with a case of measles.

13. My wife's cat was _____ in my favorite chair and refused to get up.

14. The body _____ in a corner turned out to be a pile of old clothes.

15. The Russians claimed that they were _____ the groundwork for the talks on disarmament.

B. *Use the correct form of "sit" and "set" in the following sentences.*

1. If we had known they were also at the play, we would have _____ with them.

2. Are we supposed to _____ the clock ahead an hour tonight?

3. The patient was furious after _____ in the doctor's office for two hours.

4. Lawyers claim that the case will _____ a precedent for the future.

5. Because I was not feeling well, I decided to _____ near an exit.

6. The price of the stock is _____ by the demand of the customers.

7. The delivery boy _____ the box on the front porch and left the bill.

8. The quarterback _____ on the sidelines, dejected because of his fumble.

9. Renee _____ the cups of coffee on the table and answered the telephone.

10. In our family my father used to _____ at the head of the table.

11. Because of her arthritis, it is difficult for her to get up once she has _____ down.

12. One of the duties of the operating-room nurse is to _____ out the instruments that the surgeon will use.

13. My boyfriend is _____ in the car waiting for me.

14. If the weather is pleasant, we _____ outside during our lunch break.

15. How long have you _____ in that position?

6

Review Exercise

A. Write the letter corresponding to the correct answer on the line preceding each question.

_____ 1. Which of the following statements is true:
   a.   Irregular verbs are irregular in the way their past tense and past participle forms are made.
   b.   The past tense of an irregular verb is formed by adding ''-ed'' or ''-d'' to the present tense.
   c.   The irregular verbs are rarely used in everyday speech and writing.
   d.   Most irregular verbs change in the same way.

_____ 2. What do all regular verbs add to the present tense to form the past tense and past participle forms?
   a. -ing   b. -s   c. -ies   d. -ed or -d

_____ 3. Which of the following statements is true:
   a.   In your writing you should not shift unnecessarily from one tense to another.
   b.   To describe an action that took place in the past and is still continuing, use the simple past tense.
   c.   When describing actions that occurred at the same time, it is advisable to shift frequently from one tense to another.
   d.   There are over two-hundred common tenses in the English language.

_____ 4. Which of the following statements is false:
   a.   The present tense shows present action or state of being.
   b.   The past perfect tense indicates past action occurring before another completed action in the past took place.
   c.   The present perfect tense indicates action that began in the past and is still going on.
   d.   The future tense indicates action going on now and likely to continue in the future.

_____ 5. Which of the following statements is false:

    a.   The verb "wait" is a regular verb.

    b.   "Snuck" and "swimmed" are the past tense forms of "sneak" and "swim."

    c.   To express an action that was completed at a specific time in the past, use the simple past tense.

    d.   The best way to learn irregular verb forms is to memorize them.

B. Write the letter of the correct verb form on the line before each sentence.

_____ 6. The marks on the body indicated that it had been (a. *drug;* b. *dragged;* c. *drugged)* for several blocks.

_____ 7. After I stood on the corner for two hours waiting for a bus that never came, my feet were (a. *frozed;* b. *froze;* c. *frozen).*

_____ 8. The wind had (a. *blowed;* b. *blew;* c. *blown)* so hard during the afternoon that we did not have to use our larger sails.

_____ 9. When I had a paper route in the fourth grade, I (a. *awake;* b. *awoke;* c. *awoked)* at 5:00 every morning.

_____ 10. A politician or celebrity has often (a. *thrown* b. *threw;* c. *throwed)* the first pitch at the opening of the World Series.

_____ 11. The Indians complained that the white people had (a. *break* b. *broken;* c. *broke)* too many treaties to be trusted.

_____ 12. Every car is (a. *drived;* b. *drove;* c. *driven)* over an obstacle course to test its springs and shock absorbers.

_____ 13. The pieces were carefully (a. *set;* b. *sit;* c. *sat)* in place on the chessboard.

_____ 14. Many of the immigrants found work and then (a. *brang;* b. *brought;* c. *bringed)* their relatives to America.

_____ 15. Every Friday morning promptly at eight o'clock Ms. Mather (a. *sat;* b. *sits;* c. *sets)* her trash cans on the curb and then takes her dog for a walk.

_____ 16. The catcher argued that the batter had (a. *swang;* b. *swung;* c. *swinged)* at the ball.

_____ 17. When Clarise (a. *sat;* b. *set;* c. *had sat)* her tray down, she waved to her friends across the cafeteria.

_____ 18. As the television cameras whirred, the President (a. *laid;* b. *lay;* c. *layed)* a wreath on the Tomb of the Unknown Soldier.

_____ 19. Before a passenger plane takes off, a member of the crew (a. *examines;* b. *has examined;* c. *examined*) the tires and wings of the plane with a checklist that he fills out.

_____ 20. Although Bruce has (a. *sing;* b. *sung;* c. *sang*) professionally, he still gets nervous when he appears before a group.

_____ 21. Vicki said that if she had (a. *knew;* b. *knowed;* c. *known*) what kind of party it was, she would have dressed differently.

_____ 22. The golf ball (a. *lay;* b. *laid;* c. *layed*) in a clump of weeds at the edge of a pond.

_____ 23. Johnny Longden has (a. *ride;* b. *ridden;* c. *rode*) more winners than any other jockey in history.

_____ 24. Do you remember the name of the man who first (a. *runs;* b. *ran;* c. *run*) the mile in less than four minutes?

_____ 25. Although he was a prolific composer, Edvard Grieg (a. *writes;* b. *wrote;* c. *written*) only one piano concerto.

SENTENCE COMBINING WITH GERUNDS

A gerund is the *-ing* form of a verb when it is used as a noun:

> Laughing, *according to Norman Cousins, is one of the best antidotes to illness.*

> *After trying* fasting, meditating, *and* chanting, *Meredith decided that* studying *was the best way to prepare for her driver's test.*

By adding *-ing* to a verb so that it can function as a noun, you can often combine one sentence with another:

1. *He spent his days in bed. He read. He watched television. He slept.*
(combined) *He spent his days in bed reading, watching television, and sleeping.*
2. *Greg mumbled while he took the test. It bothered the other students.*
(combined) *Greg's mumbling during the test bothered the other students.*
3. *The dog barked all night. It kept me awake.*
(combined) *The dog's barking all night kept me awake.*

Combine the following groups of sentences into single, smoother sentences by using gerunds.

1. After his retirement, Emil wants to travel. He also plans to fish and read.

2. Clare had a dream. It was to buy a new Mercedes 450SL.

3. Ray's duties at the gym were boring. He had to check out equipment, rent lockers, answer the telephone, and keep membership records.

4. Bea's travel agency has two specialties. They arrange tours to South America, and they make reservations for business travelers.

5. His boss criticized Gene yesterday. He arrives late for work, and he takes an extra half-hour for lunch.

Writing Original Sentences with Gerunds

Write ten sentences of your own, using gerunds. Underline the gerunds.

7

Compound and Complex Sentences

One of the marks of a good writer is the ability to use a variety of sentence types. The *simple* sentence is an important weapon to have in your writing arsenal, but it is limited in the ways it can be used and in the jobs it can perform. *Compound* and *complex* sentences give you additional alternatives for expressing your ideas, usually in more precise ways.

In Chapter 2 you were given a brief introduction to compound and complex sentences. In this chapter you will learn more about them, including how they are formed and punctuated and how they can make your writing more exact and interesting.

COMPOUND SENTENCES

You will recall from Chapter 2 that a simple sentence has a single subject-verb combination:

> *Lionel Richie sang.*
>
> *Lionel Richie sang and danced.*
>
> *Lionel Richie and Aretha Franklin sang.*
>
> *Lionel Richie and Aretha Franklin sang and danced.*

A *compound sentence* consists of two or more simple sentences (or *independent clauses*) containing closely related ideas and usually connected by a comma and a coordinating conjunction *(and, but, so, for, nor, or, yet)*. Below are some examples of compound sentences. Notice how each sentence consists of two independent clauses with related ideas joined with a comma and a coordinating conjunction:

> *Allan loves to cook,* **but** *he never washes his dishes.*
>
> *Nathaniel Hawthorne is my favorite writer,* **and** The Scarlet Letter *is my favorite novel.*
>
> *Richard likes Chinese food,* **so** *we took him to Peking Gardens.*

If these sentences were divided into halves, each half could stand as an independent clause or simple sentence:

> *Allan loves to cook. He never washes his dishes.*
>
> *Nathaniel Hawthorne is my favorite writer.* The Scarlet Letter *is my favorite novel.*
>
> *Richard likes Chinese food. We took him to Peking Gardens.*

By combining these simple sentences with commas and coordinating conjunctions, the results are longer, smoother compound sentences. But remember: the independent clauses in a compound sentence must contain closely related ideas, and they are usually joined with a comma and a coordinating conjunction. Never try to combine two independent clauses with a comma *only*. The result will be a *comma-splice,* a serious sentence fault. (See Chapter 8 for ways to avoid and to correct comma-splices.)

Exercise 1:

Below is a series of independent clauses, each followed by a comma. Change each clause into a compound sentence by adding a second independent clause containing a related idea and combining the two clauses with a coordinating conjunction (and, but, so, for, nor, or, *and* yet). *Try to use each of the coordinate conjunctions at least once.*

1. Scott Joplin was known for his interpretations of ragtime,_____
   _____.

2. Some of the ancient cities mentioned in the Bible are still in existence,
   _____.

3. Many writers use word processors, _____.

4. My friend Althea believes in astrology, _____.

5. By the time of John Lennon's death, the most famous of the Beatles was a millionaire, _____.

6. Coffee is probably the most popular after-dinner drink in the United States,
   _____.

7. The planet Saturn has mysterious rings around it,_____
   _____.

8. More than half of the freshmen in my state attend community colleges,
   _____.

9. In our psychology class we discussed extrasensory perception,_____
   _____.

10. The sales of cars with diesel engines have declined within the last year,
    _____.

Most independent clauses are connected by coordinate conjunctions. You may, however, use a *semicolon* **(;)** to connect the clauses if the relationship between the ideas expressed in the independent clauses is very close and obvious without a conjunction. In such cases the semicolon takes the place of both the conjunction and the comma preceding it. For example:

Hawaii is our newest state; *it was admitted to the Union in 1959.*

I love tacos and enchiladas; *they are my favorite kinds of Mexican food.*

When using a semicolon, be certain that a coordinating conjunction would not be more appropriate. Using a semicolon in the following sentence would be confusing because the relationship between the two clauses would not be clear:

(confusing)   *I have never been to France; I like French films.*

By substituting a coordinating conjunction for the semicolon, you can make clear the relationship between the clauses:

(revised)   *I have never been to France*, but *I like French films.*

Tips for Punctuating Compound Sentences

1. If the clauses in a compound sentence are connected by a coordinating conjunction, place a comma in front of the conjunction. Do not try to combine independent clauses with only a comma—the result would be a *comma-splice,* a serious sentence error. Notice the following:

(comma-splice)   *Textile mills were once the main industry in the Northeast, many of the mills are closed now.*

(correct)   *Textile mills were once the main industry in the Northeast,* but *many of the mills are closed now.*

2. If the clauses in a compound sentence are connected by a semicolon, omit the comma and the coordinate conjunction.

(incorrect)   *Calcium is important in one's diet; , and it is particularly important for pregnant women.*

(correct)   *Calcium is important to one's diet; it is particularly important for pregnant women.*

3. Do *not* place a comma before a coordinate conjunction if it does not connect independent clauses.

(incorrect)   *She was born in Vietnam, and came to Los Angeles in 1974. (The conjunction* and *does not connect two separate independent clauses.)*

(correct)   *She was born in Vietnam, and she came to Los Angeles in 1974. (Now the conjunction* and *connects two independent clauses, and therefore a comma is required.)*

(incorrect)   *Joe Louis lost his first match with Max Schmeling, but defeated him two years later.*

(correct)   *Joe Louis lost his first match with Max Schmeling, but he defeated him two years later. (Now the conjunction connects two independent clauses.)*

In Chapter 10 you will learn the rules for using the comma, including its use before *and* when it connects items in a series.

Exercise 2:

Place a comma before any conjunction connecting independent clauses in the following sentences. Some sentences do not need commas.

1. Wrigley Field in Chicago has been in use since 1916 but does not have lighting facilities for night games.

2. The producer's job is to coordinate the production financially and it is the director's job to coordinate the production artistically.

3. Martin and Connie had expected a girl but their first baby was a boy.

4. The pitcher struck out fourteen batters yet lost the game.

5. Fraternities and sororities have changed over the years but many students and faculty members still look on them with disfavor.

6. Toni earns money by baby-sitting and uses it to pay for her car insurance and driving expenses.

7. His headache was worse yet he managed to smile.

8. Elizabeth received her degree in May and she began work as a newswriter for a local television station.

9. In the last election many voters either did not vote or wrote ''none of the above'' on their ballots and thereby expressed their frustration.

10. Either he has traveled around the world or he has an incredible imagination.

Reminders for Compound Sentences

* A compound sentence consists of two or more independent clauses connected by a semicolon or a coordinating conjunction (a word like *and, but,* and *or*).
* If the clauses in a compound sentence are connected by a coordinating conjunction, place a comma in front of the conjunction.
* Never try to combine independent clauses with a comma *only*. You must use a comma *and* a coordinating conjunction.

COMPLEX SENTENCES

Because their ideas can be shifted around to produce different emphases or rhythms, *complex* sentences offer the writer more variety than do simple sentences. Complex sentences are often more precise than compound sentences because a compound sentence must treat two ideas equally. Complex sentences, on the other hand, can establish more exact relationships. In Chapter 2 you learned that there are two kinds of clauses: *independent* and *dependent.* An independent clause can stand alone and form a complete sentence. A dependent clause, however, cannot stand alone. Even though it has a subject and verb, it fails to express a complete thought. It must be attached to an independent clause in order to form a grammatically complete sentence.

You can recognize dependent clauses by the kinds of words that introduce them, making them dependent. The technical terms for these introducing words are *subordinating conjunctions* and *relative pronouns.* Notice that each of the following dependent clauses begins with such a word:

Although *Dale is very shy*

If *we were to drive all night*

Because *the drainage canal was filled with water*

Who *had studied at the University of Texas*

Which *barely reached his shoulders*

Although these clauses contain subjects and verbs, they do not express complete ideas. By adding an independent clause, however, you can change each word group into a complete, grammatically correct *complex* sentence:

Although Dale is very shy, he delivered his address without any problems.

If we were to drive all night, we could reach Terre Haute by noon.

Because the drainage canal was filled with water, the street was soon flooded.

Our guide in Tokyo was a young woman who had studied at the University of Texas.

The fence, which barely reached his shoulders, had once been a barrier against the neighbor's cows.

NOTE: *A dependent clause is usually followed by a comma when it begins a sentence. If an independent clause comes first, no comma is needed.*

The following list contains the most common dependent clause introducing words. Whenever a clause begins with one of them (unless it is a question), it is a dependent clause in a complex sentence.

after	because
although	before
as, as if	how
as though	if

in order that	what, whatever
once	when, whenever
since	where, wherever
so that	whether
than	which, whichever
that	while
though	who, whose, whoever
unless	whom

Exercise 3:

If the italicized clause in each sentence is a dependent clause, *write "dep" on the line preceding the sentence. If it is an* independent clause, *write "ind" on the line.*

_____ 1. Some of our country's most successful people went to small colleges *that you may not have heard of.*

_____ 2. The Maori are Polynesians *who settled in New Zealand over one thousand years ago.*

_____ 3. *Sam complained* that his expensive watchband was turning his wrist green.

_____ 4. Bill's new camera can take pictures from the light of a birthday candle, *and its pictures are crisp and clear.*

_____ 5. *Because she did not know the language,* Jan could not read the directions to the museum.

_____ 6. Meteorologists now forecast rain in terms of percentages *because such predictions are more accurate.*

_____ 7. Before you buy a microwave oven, *you should take a course in microwave cooking.*

_____ 8. The cannon shot *that smashed into Fort Sumter* started the most awesome war in America's history.

_____ 9. *If you visit Quebec,* you will hear the French language spoken daily.

_____ 10. Ernie installed a smoke alarm in his home, *and the premium on his insurance policy was reduced as a result.*

Exercise 4:

Add an independent clause to each of the following dependent clauses, thereby creating a complex sentence.

1. Although I should have known better, _____.

2. _____ because he gave me good advice.

3. Before Arthur knew it, _____.

4. If proper precautions are taken, _____.

5. _____ that it was impossible.

6. Unless you make careful plans, _____.

7. _____ until women were allowed to vote.

8. _____ when it was least expected.

9. _____ who receives the fewest votes.

10. Since we were both too tired to go, _____.

Reminders for Complex Sentences

---

* Dependent clauses begin with words like ''after,'' ''if,'' ''although,'' and other words on the list on pages 115-16. A dependent clause cannot stand alone—it must be combined with an independent clause in order to be complete.
* When a dependent clause begins a sentence, it is followed by a comma. If the independent clause comes first, no comma is needed.
* A complex sentence is one that contains a dependent clause.

Three Kinds of Dependent Clauses

Now that you can recognize dependent clauses in complex sentences, it is time to take a closer look at them so that you will know how to use them correctly and make your own sentences more interesting and mature.

All dependent clauses share three traits: they all have a subject and a verb, they begin with a dependent clause introducing word, and they must be combined with independent clauses to form a complete sentence. So much for the similarities; let us now consider the differences among them.

Dependent clauses can be used in sentences in three different ways: as adverbs, as adjectives, and as nouns. Consequently, we label them *adverb clauses, adjective clauses,* and *noun clauses.*

ADVERB CLAUSES   Adverb clauses act as adverbs in a sentence—they modify verbs, adjectives, and adverbs. Like single-word adverbs, they can be recognized by the questions they answer. They tell *when, where, why, how,* or *under what conditions something happens.* They can also be recognized because they begin with subordinating conjunctions. In the following sentences the adverb clauses are italicized:

> *When I was a senior in high school,* I broke my arm playing basketball.
> (The adverb clause tells *when.)*

Jack's dog follows him *wherever he goes.* (The adverb clause tells *where.*)

Because she could speak Spanish fluently, Edith was hired as an interpreter at the courthouse. (The adverb clause tells *why.*)

She threw the shot put *as if it were a tennis ball.* (The adverb clause tells *how.*)

I would help you *if I could.* (The adverb clause tells *under what conditions.*)

Adverb clauses can usually be moved around in a sentence. In the first sentence above, for example, the adverb clause can be placed at the end of the sentence without affecting its basic meaning: I broke my arm playing basketball *when I was a senior in high school.* Notice that an adverb clause is followed by a comma when it comes at the beginning of a sentence; when it comes at the end of a sentence, it is not preceded by a comma.

Exercise 5:

Underline all of the adverb clauses in the following sentences, and supply any missing commas.

1. The waiting room of the airport was full of angry passengers because the plane was three hours late.

2. Before you apply for a job you should know something about the company.

3. After finding the wallet where I had left it I returned in embarrassment to the restaurant.

4. Although she expected a raise she had to settle for a promotion.

5. Chrysler's production rate increased more than Ford's did.

6. Unless the current demographic statistics alter drastically one-fourth of all Americans will be over sixty in the year 2000.

7. As the orchestra played the official song of the beauty pageant the contestants smiled and waved at the audience.

8. Doak played professional football until he was injured.

9. If literacy were a requirement for the right to vote many present voters could not vote.

10. While the workers took down the speakers' platform and tore down the placards and decorations the crowds drifted slowly away.

ADJECTIVE CLAUSES   Adjective clauses modify nouns and pronouns in a complex sentence. Like all clauses, they have subjects and verbs. But as dependent clauses, they must be attached to independent clauses to express complete ideas and to form grammatically complete sentences.

Most adjective clauses begin with the relative pronouns *which, whom, that, who,* and *whose,* but a few are introduced by *when, where, why,* and *how.* Adjective clauses usually follow immediately the noun or pronoun they modify. In the following sentences the adjective clauses are italicized:

Anne Frank's diary, *which she began in 1942,* was terminated by her capture and death in 1945. (The adjective clause modifies *diary.)*

Gilda's father, *whom you met last night,* is from Baltimore. (The adjective clause modifies *father.)*

Many of the monuments *that have survived in ancient Egypt through thousands of years* were achieved at a terrible cost in human suffering and death. (The adjective clause modifies *monuments.)*

Any pitcher *who deliberately hits a batter* will be ejected. (The adjective clause modifies *pitcher.)*

Drivers *whose cars are left unattended* will receive citations. (The adjective clause modifies *Drivers.)*

Exercise 6:

Underline the adjective clauses in the following sentences. In the line preceding each sentence, write the noun or pronoun modified by the clause.

_____   1. Constance told me about the wealthy prince whom she met while on a vacation in Europe.

_____   2. The socks that did not have mates were thrown away.

_____   3. The bargain Swiss watch that I bought in Tijuana turned out to be a fake.

_____   4. Every newspaper has a morgue which is the newspaper's library.

_____   5. My neighbor, who is a retired pharmacist, collects punk rock records.

_____   6. A speaker from the International Red Cross told us about floods that have devastated the towns and villages of central India.

_____   7. A parent whose children attend the school protested the closing of the cafeteria.

_____   8. Orson Welles wrote and produced a radio drama in the 1930s which terrified thousands of listeners.

_____ 9. Hamlet is the character who provokes our interest.

_____ 10. An old cigar box which served as his safe was found under the bed.

PUNCTUATING ADJECTIVE CLAUSES   Perhaps you noticed that the adjective clause in the fifth sentence above and those in the first two examples on page 119 *(which she began in 1942* and *whom you met last night)* were set off by commas. That is because they are *nonessential* (or *nonrestrictive*) adjective clauses. Nonessential clauses merely give additional information about the nouns or pronouns they modify. If we were to omit the adjective clauses in the two examples on page 119 cited above, they would still convey their central idea:

> *Anne Frank's diary,* which she began in 1942, *was terminated by her capture and death in 1945. (The adjective clause provides nonessential information.)*

> *Anne Frank's diary was terminated by her capture and death in 1945. (Although the adjective clause has been removed, we still can identify the subject.)*

> *Gilda's father,* whom you met last night, *is from Baltimore. (The fact that you met her father last night is nonessential.)*

> *Gilda's father is from Baltimore. (By identifying the subject as* Gilda's father, *the writer is able to delete the nonessential clause without destroying the sentence.)*

The punctuation rule for *nonessential* adjective clauses is easy: they should be set off by commas. Essential clauses—those needed to identify the subject—should not be set off by commas. In the third example on page 119, the omission of the adjective clause would be confusing:

> *Many of the monuments were achieved at a terrible cost in human suffering and death.*

This is a complete sentence, but the adjective clause is essential because it tells the reader *which* monuments the writer is referring to. Therefore, it is needed to identify the subject and is not set off with commas:

> *Many of the monuments* that have survived in ancient Egypt through thousands of years *were achieved at a terrible cost in human suffering and death.*

The punctuation rule for essential adjective clauses, therefore, is simple: they should *not* be set off by commas. Chapter 10 gives additional examples concerning the punctuation of essential and nonessential clauses.

Reminders for Punctuating Adjective Clauses

---

* If the adjective clause is essential to the meaning of the sentence, do *not* set it off with commas.
* If the adjective clause is *not* essential to the meaning of the sentence, set it off with commas.

Exercise 7:

Underline all adjective clauses in the following sentences and supply any missing commas.

1. Sensors that were taped to the patient's head relayed responses on a graph that was in another room.

2. My cousin Bridget who lives in Dublin speaks Gaelic, a language that is spoken by only twenty percent of the Irish.

3. Any musician who accepts a position with the symphony is on probation for the first six months.

4. My sister Anne who is two years younger than I is two inches taller.

5. The pigeons that roost in the trees behind my house will eat anything that I throw on the ground.

6. The novelist Ernest Hemingway who was born in Illinois spent much of his life in foreign countries.

7. The Raiders who were favored to win the championship have gotten off to a poor start this season.

8. The person who answered the door turned out to be my future husband.

9. Catchers who are left-handed are a rarity in baseball.

10. The May 1 concert of the Who which had been sold out for two months was canceled because of the illness of two members of the group.

11. Jobs that pay well and do not require much work are difficult to find.

12. The earthquake that leveled San Francisco in 1906 killed thousands of people and did millions of dollars of damage.

13. Those who have red hair and freckles usually sunburn easily.

14. My favorite tennis shoes which are grass-stained and falling apart have served me well over the years.

15. Ms. Pennington who was my fourth-grade teacher worked as a clown in a circus during the summer.

NOUN CLAUSES Noun clauses do the same things in sentences that single nouns do: they function as subjects, objects, or subject complements. Unlike adjective clauses and adverb clauses, noun clauses do not join independent clauses to form complete sentences. Instead, they replace one of the nouns in independent clauses. As a result, they function as subjects, objects, or subject complements of independent clauses. They are usually introduced by such words as *that, who, what, where, how,* and *why.*

As a subject:	What he said on that occasion *will always be remembered.*
As a direct object:	*Sally thought* that his idea was good.
As the object of a preposition:	*The referee was angered by* what the player said.
As a subject complement:	*The Christmas present was* what he wanted.

Exercise 8:

In the line preceding each sentence identify the italicized noun clause according to the way it is used in the sentence, using the following letters:
a. subject   b. direct object   c. object of preposition   d. subject complement

_____ 1. We were excited by *what Harvey told us.*

_____ 2. The pickpocket denied *that he had taken Margaret's purse.*

_____ 3. *That the earth is flat* has not been proved to my satisfaction.

_____ 4. Most of us realized *what was happening.*

_____ 5. Charley's present was *what he had always wanted.*

_____ 6. Because of his confusion, Carl could not remember *what had happened the night before.*

_____ 7. *How my father can watch a baseball game, work a crossword puzzle, and talk to us at the same time* amazes me.

_____ 8. I have the feeling that this was *where we came in.*

_____ 9. Chris said that he would never forget *what he saw that cold winter morning forty years ago.*

_____ 10. Rita had very little interest in *what she was reading.*

Exercise 9:

Underline the noun clauses in the following sentences.

1. The voters believed that a state lottery would help finance the public schools.

2. Everyone in the audience knew how the movie would end.

3. What he said and what he did were two different things.

4. Whatever profits are made will be donated to the local orphanage.

5. The surprise is that Helen decided to marry him despite his temper.

7

Review Exercise

A. *Identify each of the following sentences according to its structure.*
a. *simple*   b. *compound*   c. *complex*

_____ 1. The arsenic level in the water was almost double the safe limit, and an asbestos dump was two miles down the road.

_____ 2. Americans must constantly be on the alert to any infringements of their basic constitutional rights, according to the lawyer.

_____ 3. Many farmers like to hire migrant workers because they work hard and are reliable.

_____ 4. As a young man, Billy liked horses; today, he works as a trainer at the race track.

_____ 5. Although the judge did not cite him for contempt, he was subsequently arrested for drunkenness.

_____ 6. According to anthropologists, the human shape will change in coming centuries.

_____ 7. If the fire alarm is not repaired within ten days, the authorities will close the restaurant.

_____ 8. The conversion of farmland to suburban shopping centers, new highways, parks, dwellings, and other nonagricultural uses affects the amount of land available for food production.

_____ 9. According to a survey by the state Department of Transportation, independent truckers carry a sizeable portion of the country's goods.

_____ 10. Many drivers who are on the road today do not have insurance or a driver's license.

B. *Each of the following sentences contains one or two blanks. If a comma should be inserted in* one or both *blanks, write "a" on the line in front of the sentences; if no commas should be inserted, write "b."*

_____ 11. Every male _____ who was between the ages of eighteen and forty-five _____ was required to register for the draft.

_____ 12. Siberian cranes _____ which come from the tundras of the Soviet Union _____ are among the world's most endangered migratory birds.

_____ 13. The federal tobacco program _____ which guarantees farmers a minimum price for their crop _____ is facing increasing opposition in Washington.

_____ 14. A study _____ which predicts a warming trend in the earth's atmosphere _____ was recently issued by a team of scientists in Canada.

_____ 15. The city planner predicted a time _____ when housing developers would create houses that produce their own power and energy.

_____ 16. People _____ who are fair skinned _____ should use a suntan lotion that lets the ultraviolet rays in slowly and gradually.

_____ 17. Richard Burton _____ who attended Oxford _____ acted in the movies as well as on the stage.

_____ 18. Jimmy Carter _____ whose administration established diplomatic ties with China _____ wrote a history of his presidency.

_____ 19. An odor _____ that was similar to the smell of burning rubber _____ filled the automobile.

_____ 20. The negotiators proposed an international treaty _____ that would ban weapons of any kind from being sent into the earth's orbit.

_____ 21. It was the disagreement over seniority rights that led to the collapse of the negotiating session _____ and the threat of a strike.

_____ 22. After they abandoned their sinking ship _____ the sailors began to swim toward the shore.

_____ 23. Before buying a used car you should ask a mechanic to look at it; _____ he can often spot hidden defects and problems.

_____ 24. Mardi Gras festivities contribute much to the economy of New Orleans _____ and help popularize the city's attractions.

_____ 25. When semiconductors and transistors went into mass production _____ the price of calculators plummeted.

SENTENCE COMBINING WITH ADJECTIVE CLAUSES

In this chapter (pages 119-20) you learned that adjective clauses modify nouns and pronouns in complex sentences. Most adjective clauses begin with the relative pronouns *that, who, whom, whose,* and *which.* One of the most effective ways of ridding your writing of choppy sentences is to combine them with other sentences by using an adjective clause.

1. *The noise frightened me. It was a sonic boom from a jet plane.*
(combined)   *The noise* that frightened me *was a sonic boom from a jet plane.*
2. *The Midland Bank was the largest in our city. It has gone into bankruptcy.*
(combined)   *The Midland Bank,* which was the largest in our city, *has gone into bankruptcy.*
3. *Doctor John Lilly is a neurophysiologist. He has spent years trying to teach dolphins to speak.*
(combined)   *Doctor John Lilly is a neurophysiologist* who has spent years trying to teach dolphins to speak.

Remember that *nonessential* adjective clauses are set off by commas and *essential* adjective clauses are *not* set off by commas. Review pages 120–21 if necessary for the rules on punctuating adjective clauses.

Combine the following pairs of sentences by changing one of the sentences to an adjective clause. Remember to set off nonessential clauses with commas.

1. Paul Revere is famous for his midnight ride. He was a silversmith in Boston.

2. Zubin Mehta is the conductor of the New York Philharmonic Orchestra. He is a native of India.

3. The soap opera actor was asked for autographs. We recognized him.

4. I received a call from my Aunt Marie last week. I had not heard from her for ten years.

5. You raised several points last night at the meeting. They were interesting and helpful.

Writing Original Sentences with Adjective Clauses

Write ten original sentences, using adjective clauses. Underline the clauses and remember to set off nonessential clauses with commas.

8

Correcting Sentence Fragments, Run-On Sentences, and Comma-Splices

The purpose of writing is to communicate facts, ideas, and feelings in a clear and effective manner. If we make serious mistakes in sentence structure or grammar, our readers are confused and irritated, and communication fails. This chapter deals with ways to remedy three serious kinds of errors a writer can make: *sentence fragments, run-on sentences,* and *comma-splices.*

SENTENCE FRAGMENTS

A *sentence* is a group of words that contains at least one independent clause. It has a subject and a verb, and it conveys a certain sense of completeness. A *sentence fragment,* on the other hand, is a group of words that lacks an independent clause. Although it looks like a sentence because it begins with a capital letter and ends with a period or other end punctuation, it leaves the reader ''hanging,'' waiting for more to follow.

Sentence fragments are common in conversation, particularly in responses to what someone else has said or as additions to something we have just said. Their meanings and missing parts are usually clear because of the context of the conversation and the speaker's gestures. In writing, however, it is best to avoid sentence fragments. Although professional writers occasionally use them for special effects, fragments usually suggest that the writer is careless and unable to formulate a complete thought.

One of the best ways to avoid sentence fragments is to read your written work *aloud.* Your voice will often detect an incomplete sentence. Another tip: Don't be fooled by the length of a so-called sentence. A long string of words without an independent clause is still a sentence fragment, despite its length. Here is an example of such a fragment:

> *The closing ceremony of the Los Angeles Olympics, with thousands of athletes from across the globe, almost 100,000 spectators in the Coloseum, a dazzling array of fireworks, a laser-beam show, the appearance of a flying saucer suspended from a helicopter, and climaxed by the appearance of Lionel Richie singing a song with special lyrics he wrote for the occasion.*

At first glance this ''sentence'' is complete—after all, it begins with a capitalized word and concludes with a period. Despite its length, however, it is a sentence fragment because it does not contain an independent clause and therefore cannot convey a complete thought.

The following list contains the most common types of fragments that people write:

1. *Prepositional phrase fragments*
2. *Infinitive fragments*
3. *Participle fragments*
4. *Noun fragments*
5. *Dependent clause fragments*

By understanding each type of fragment, you can eliminate them from your writing. Now we will look at the various types of sentence fragments and the ways to correct them.

Phrases as Fragments

One of the most common kinds of sentence fragments is the *phrase*. (A *phrase*, you recall, is a group of words lacking a subject and a verb and acting as a single part of speech within a sentence.) *Prepositional phrases, infinitive phrases,* and *participle phrases* are often confused with complete sentences.

THE PREPOSITIONAL PHRASE AS A FRAGMENT   A prepositional phrase never contains a subject and a verb. Therefore, it can never stand alone as a sentence. The following sentences are followed by prepositional phrases masquerading as sentences:

(fragment)   *The Italian composer Verdi continued to write great operas.* Despite his advanced age.
(fragment)   *One of the great backs of football, Gale Sayers set several scoring records.* In his rookie year with the Chicago Bears.
(fragment)   *After delaying it several weeks, Jeff finally began his term paper.* On the subject of religious cults in America.

Because prepositional phrases are parts of sentences, the best way to correct this kind of fragment is to join it with the sentence it belongs to. Notice how the fragments above were eliminated when they were joined to the preceding sentences:

(sentence)   *The Italian composer Verdi continued to write great operas despite his advanced age.*
(sentence)   *One of the great backs of football, Gale Sayers set several scoring records in his rookie year with the Chicago Bears.*
(sentence)   *After delaying it several weeks, Jeff finally began his term paper on the subject of religious cults in America.*

THE INFINITIVE PHRASE AS A FRAGMENT   An infinitive is the "to" form of the verb: *to help, to see, to start,* and so on. Many fragments are the result of the writer trying to use an infinitive as the verb in a sentence:

(fragment)   To serve as a reminder to succeeding generations. *The cell in which he was jailed was established as a memorial.*
(fragment)   *Because of the age of my Chevrolet, I decided that it was too expensive.* To overhaul the car, put in a new transmission and valves, and buy new tires.
(fragment)   *It was a shattering experience.* To see with our own eyes the damage caused by the bombs.

Most fragments consisting of infinitives can be corrected by combining them with the sentence they belong to. Occasionally, however, it is necessary to rewrite the fragment or its independent clause:

(sentence) *To serve as a reminder to succeeding generations, the cell in which he was jailed was established as a memorial.*

(sentence) *Because of the age of my Chevrolet, I decided that it was too expensive to overhaul the car, put in a new transmission and valves, and buy new tires.*

(sentence) *It was a shattering experience to see with our own eyes the damage caused by the bombs.*

THE PARTICIPLE PHRASE AS A FRAGMENT   The present participle is the ''-ing'' form of the verb: *helping, seeing, starting, walking.* Present participles can never serve as verbs in a sentence unless they have helping verbs with them (see Chapters 1, 2, 3, and 6). Like the infinitive, the participial phrase is often confused with the main verb in a sentence, and the result is a fragment:

(fragment) Growing up in a large, poor family in the Appalachian Mountains. *He realized that a college education would be an impossibility.*

(fragment) *Madame Tussaud's Wax Museum is a popular tourist attraction in London.* Featurng likenesses of historical personages reproduced in lifelike poses.

(fragment) Exercising every day, cutting down on calories, and avoiding ice cream and other desserts. *I was able to lose twenty pounds last summer.*

Fragments like these can be corrected by attaching them to the independent clauses preceding or following them:

(sentence) *Growing up in a large, poor family in the Appalachian Mountains, he realized that a college education would be an impossibility.*

(sentence) *Madame Tussaud's Wax Museum is a popular tourist attraction in London, featuring likenesses of historical personages reproduced in lifelike poses.*

(sentence) *Exercising every day, cutting down on calories, and avoiding ice cream and other desserts, I was able to lose twenty pounds last summer.*

Another way to correct fragments like these is to supply them with their missing subjects or verbs (or both):

(sentence) *He grew up in a large, poor family in the Appalachian Mountains, and he realized that a college education would be an*

impossibility. (Supplying the missing subject and verb and combining the fragment with another sentence)

(sentence)   *Madame Tussaud's Wax Museum is a popular tourist attraction
in London. It features likenesses of historical personages reproduced in lifelike poses.* (Supplying the missing subject and verb
and creating two separate sentences)

(sentence)   *Because I exercised every day, cut down on calories, and avoided
ice cream and other desserts, I was able to lose twenty pounds last
summer.* (Changing the fragment into a dependent clause and
changing the sentence into a complex sentence)

Exercise 1:

*Some of the following word groups contain sentence fragments. Underline the frag-
ment, writing on the line the kind of fragment it is. Then correct the fragment by one
of the methods explained above. If the group does not contain a fragment, write "C."*

Example: Barbara enjoyed her job at the restaurant𝗑.

participial phrase   **e**
                            𝐄specially greeting and seating the customers.

_____ 1. Forgetting that her keys were in the ignition. Beth locked the car.

Infinitive 2. To seek a cure for depression and to determine its causes. A group of
researchers had been meeting in town all week.

_____ 3. Mark had a dream when he was a young man. To be a millionaire by the
age of thirty.

_____ 4. Uncle Harry continues to be in good health. Through exercise and good
                                                          Preposition
eating habits.

_____ 5. Staring out the window at the clouds. Marie thought of her home in
Munich and the friends she had left.

_____ 6. Walter spends most of his afternoons in retirement. Puttering around in
his garden and taking walks to the local park.

_____ 7. The speech course promised its students confidence and the ability to
speak extemporaneously. On any subject or topic.

_____ 8. Slipping, falling, and sliding down the slope. Kent finally made it to the
bottom of the steep hill.

_____ 9. Because of her attitude and her willingness to adapt to new situations.
Margie was given a promotion after six months.

_____ 10. Believing that the threat of a flood had passed, the villagers returned to
their homes.

Noun Fragments

Another type of fragment is a noun followed by a modifier with no main verb:

(fragment) *William Harvey, the English physiologist credited with discovering the circulation of blood in the human body.*

(fragment) *The volcano, hurling ash and steam some 60,000 feet into the sky.*

(fragment) *The magnificent view from the air, with the mountains in the distant eastern horizon, the ocean faintly visible to the north, and the lush green farms directly below.*

Most noun fragments can be corrected by supplying the missing verbs:

(sentence) *William Harvey* was *the English physiologist credited with discovering the circulation of blood in the human body.*

(sentence) *The volcano* hurled *ash and steam some 60,000 feet into the sky.*

(sentence) *The view from the air, with the mountains in the distant eastern horizon, the ocean faintly visible to the north, and the lush green farms directly below,* was *magnificent.*

Dependent Clauses as Fragments

Dependent clauses cannot stand alone as complete sentences. But because they contain subjects and verbs, they often end up as fragments. Dependent clauses can be spotted by the kinds of words that introduce them: subordinate conjunctions like *after, although, as, because,* and *if* or relative pronouns like *who, which,* and *that* (see page 115 for a list of words that introduce dependent clauses).

A dependent clause set off as a complete sentence can be corrected by combining it with the independent clause preceding or following it. Another method is to delete the subordinating conjunction or relative pronoun, thereby converting it to an independent clause.

(fragment) *Veronica developed an allergy.* Which the doctor could not diagnose.

(revised) *Veronica developed an allergy which the doctor could not diagnose.*

(fragment) *Harry Truman pulled off a stunning upset victory in the 1948 presidential election.* Although everyone had predicted that Thomas E. Dewey of New York would win.

(revised) *Harry Truman pulled off a stunning upset victory in the 1948 presidential election, although everyone had predicted that Thomas E. Dewey of New York would win.*

Some Tips for Avoiding Sentence Fragments

✱1. Read your paper aloud. You will usually be able to hear whether or not you have written a fragment.

✱2. Be sure that every word group has a subject and a verb.

✱3. Look for the most common types of fragments:
   *Phrase fragments (prepositional phrases, *to* and *-ing* phrases)
   *Noun fragments (a noun followed by modifiers but without a verb)
   *Dependent-clause fragments

✱ Exercise 2:

Correct any sentence fragments in the following word groups, using any of the methods explained above. If the sentence is correct, write "C" in front of it.

1. Matt was uncomfortable in his new suit. Because his trousers did not fit.

2. Thousands of foreign families come to Disneyland every summer as tourists. And return to their homes with a strange view of the United States.

3. Many of those who criticize the Miss America Pageant. They believe that it emphasizes outdated or sexist values.

4. The bomb squad was called to the airport to detonate a package. Containing a mysterious green liquid that turned out to be a detergent.

5. Many of the young professional women postponing decisions to have children until they are further along in their careers.

6. Although certified to teach chemistry and physics in high school and possessing an advanced degree in Russian.

7. Remarkable gains have been achieved by minorities who took the SAT and ACT tests last year.

8. The psychological effects, according to insurance company studies, of living alone, and their relationship to mortality rates.

9. One of the benefits of a course in art, particularly in evaluating modern sculpture and painting.

10. Ansel Adams' most famous photographs, taken in Yosemite National Park and in other areas of striking natural beauty.

RUN-ON SENTENCES

A *run-on sentence* is just the opposite of a sentence fragment. It is a group of words that *looks* like one sentence and is *punctuated* like one sentence, but is actually two sentences run together without punctuation. Normally, of course, two or more independent clauses are separated by a coordinating conjunction or a semicolon. But if the conjunction or the semicolon is omitted, the result is a run-on sentence.

Run-on sentences can be corrected in four ways:

1. By inserting a comma and a conjunction *(and, but, for, or, yet, so)* between the independent clauses.

(run-on)   *Years ago I took calculus I have forgotten practically all I once knew about the subject.*

(revised)   *Years ago I took calculus, **but** I have forgotten practically all I once knew about the subject.*

2. By changing one of the independent clauses into a dependent clause.

(run-on)   *In the first inning we were winning eight to one two innings later we were losing twelve to eight.*

(revised)   *Although we were winning eight to one in the first inning, two innings later we were losing twelve to eight.*

3. By inserting a semicolon between the two independent clauses.

(run-on)   *Ignoring the advice of my wife I bought a boat for the last two months I have spent every spare minute scraping paint.*

(revised)   *Ignoring the advice of my wife, I bought a boat; for the last two months I have spent every spare minute scraping paint.*

4. By using a period or other end punctuation between the independent clauses, making them two separate sentences.

(run-on)   *The Gideon decision is one of the landmark cases of the U.S. Supreme Court it grants all poor defendants the right to counsel.*

(revised)   *The Gideon decision is one of the landmark cases of the U.S. Supreme Court. It grants all poor defendants the right to counsel.*

Some Tips for Avoiding Run-On Sentences

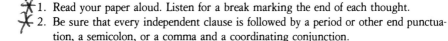

1. Read your paper aloud. Listen for a break marking the end of each thought.
2. Be sure that every independent clause is followed by a period or other end punctuation, a semicolon, or a comma and a coordinating conjunction.

Exercise 3:

Using any of the methods explained above, correct any run-on sentences in the following word groups. If a sentence is correct, mark it "C."

1. Being left-handed can be helpful for some people it can be an advantage in sports, for example.

2. Bilingual education programs enrolled millions of students in elementary schools within the last year, however, these programs have been attacked by some groups.

3. Last summer I called several local sporting goods stores in order to find a job none of them needed part-time help.

4. The idea of Atlantis has fascinated people since the time of the ancient Greeks no evidence for its existence has been unearthed.

5. A horticulturist in Cleveland was arrested for growing marijuana in his backyard he told officers he had not recognized the plants.

6. Mexico and the United States have sponsored a meeting to discuss fishing rights for their respective fishing fleets.

7. A shower of falling stars and meteors is expected late tonight it can be seen in the southeastern sky.

8. Owning a pet implies a commitment beyond providing food and medical care many pet owners, however, do not accept the responsibilities.

9. The best-seller list contained several mysteries and "how-to" books biographies of movie stars were also listed.

10. A computer listing of missing children has been established throughout the country authorities hope that it will help parents find their children.

COMMA-SPLICES

A comma-splice consists of two independent clauses connected ("spliced") by only a comma instead of being joined with a comma *and* a coordinating conjunction or with a semicolon. A comma-splice is only slightly less irritating to a reader than the run-on sentence: the writer made some attempt (although mistakenly) to separate two independent clauses. Nevertheless, a comma-splice is a serious error in sentence construction because it is difficult to read. Furthermore, it suggests, like the fragment and run-on sentence, that the writer cannot formulate or recognize a single, complete thought.

Comma-splices can be corrected in the same ways as run-on sentences:

1. By using a period or other end punctuation between the independent clauses, making them two sentences.

(comma-splice) *For many years sociologists referred to the United States as a "melting pot," that concept has been replaced by the term "pluralistic society."*

(revised) *For many years sociologists referred to the United States as a "melting pot." That concept has been replaced by the term "pluralistic society."*

2. By inserting a comma and a conjunction between the independent clauses.

(comma-splice) *Dennis enrolled in a course in ballroom dancing, now all of the women want to dance with him.*

(revised) *Dennis enrolled in a course in ballroom dancing, and now all of the women want to dance with him.*

3. By inserting a semicolon between the two independent clauses.

(comma-splice) *Jack told me the test was difficult, he was right.*

(revised) *Jack told me the test was difficult; he was right*

4. By changing one of the independent clauses into a dependent clause.

(comma-splice) *Mike studied classical music at a conservatory in New York, he plays drums in a rock group.*

(revised) *Although Mike studied classical music at a conservatory in New York, he plays drums in a rock group.*

Some Tips for Avoiding Comma-Splices

---

* 1. Do not use a comma alone to separate your sentences.
* 2. Read your sentence aloud. When you signal a new thought, use a period or other end punctuation, a semicolon, or a comma *and* a coordinate conjunction.

Exercise 4:

Using any of the methods explained above, correct any comma-splices in the following word groups. If a sentence is correct, mark it "C."

1. The horse picked its way carefully across the stream, it seemed to be feeling the rocks with its hoofs.

2. Hillary opened a savings account, but she had to withdraw most of it within a week.

3. Bored with school, Roger decided to join the Army, he soon missed his buddies.

4. Tourists who come to the West Coast during the winter months are called ''snow birds'' by Californians, many of whom are former ''snow birds'' themselves.

5. Most classrooms do not have desks for left-handed students, in fact most tools are for right-handed people.

6. According to some geneticists, personality traits can be inherited, although it cannot be proved, it is a controversial theory.

7. An onion a day keeps everyone away, an apple a day keeps the doctor away.

8. Both teams were exhausted after the double-header, even the fans were tired.

9. The car, an experimental model, had only three cylinders, and therefore it was economical to operate.

10. Robin lived too far away to drive to the high school reunion, she called the class chairperson to express her regrets.

Comma-Splices and Conjunctive Adverbs

Some comma-splices are the result of the writer's confusing a *conjunctive adverb* with a coordinating conjunction. A conjunctive adverb is a kind of connecting word that looks like a conjunction but is actually an adverb. Conjunctive adverbs are words like the following:

accordingly, also, besides, consequently, furthermore, hence, however, moreover, nevertheless, nonetheless, otherwise, therefore

When one of these words appears *within* an independent clause, it is usually set off by commas:

(correct)　*It was obvious from her face,* **however,** *that she was disappointed.*
(correct)　*I believe,* **nevertheless,** *that Vince will continue to play.*
(correct)　*Japan and Ireland,* **moreover,** *also plan to sign the treaty.*

When a conjunctive adverb appears *between* main clauses, it must be preceded by a semicolon (and often followed by a comma) or a period. If the semicolon or period is omitted, the result is a comma-splice:

(comma-splice) *At one time Portugal belonged to Spain, however, since 1640 it has been a separate, independent nation.*

(correct) *At one time Portugal belonged to Spain*; **however,** *since 1640 it has been a separate, independent nation.*

(correct) *At one time Portugal belonged to Spain.* **However,** *since 1640 it has been a separate, independent nation.*

(comma-splice) *The Internal Revenue Service has been forced to lay off thousands of its employees, consequently, it has audited fewer income-tax returns in recent years.*

(correct) *The Internal Revenue Service has been forced to lay off thousands of its employees; consequently, it has audited fewer income-tax returns in recent years.*

(correct) *The Internal Revenue Service has been forced to lay off thousands of its employees. Consequently, it has audited fewer income-tax returns in recent years.*

Remember: Conjunctive adverbs are not conjunctions and can never be used by themselves to link clauses or sentences.

Exercise 5:

Correct any comma-splices in the following groups of words. Use any of the methods presented above. If a sentence is correct, mark it "C."

1. The OPEC nations have raised the price of oil, therefore, the price of gasoline in this country will probably rise.

2. The game of chess goes back to ancient times, in fact, its exact origin is unknown.

3. Cleveland has a large ethnic population, consequently, several languages and cultures exist side by side.

4. Harold just made the last payment on his car, furthermore, he just paid off his loan at the credit union.

5. Con wanted to attend a college near his home, therefore, he attended the local community college.

6. I paid five dollars for the taxi fare and ten dollars for the tickets, otherwise, I would not have stayed for the second act of the play.

7. Libya, on the other hand, refuses to accept responsibility for the incident.

8. Andy never reads a book, moreover, he is proud of it.

9. Entrance requirements for medical school have been tightened, as a result, many prospective doctors are working harder to keep up their grade point averages.

10. You have not completely convinced me, nevertheless, I will accept your decision to drop out of school.

8

Review Exercise

A. Select the letter corresponding to the correct answer.

_____ 1. A group of words lacking an independent clause is:

    a. a sentence fragment

    b. a compound sentence

    c. a complex sentence

_____ 2. A run-on sentence:

    a. is a sentence that is too long

    b. can be corrected by inserting a comma

    c. lacks a conjunction or semicolon between independent clauses

_____ 3. A comma-splice can be corrected by:

    a. separating the clauses with a comma

    b. putting a period at the end of the last clause

    c. connecting its independent clauses with a comma and a coordinating conjunction

_____ 4. Which of the following is a conjunctive adverb:

    a. nevertheless b. yet c. but

_____ 5. Which of the following statements is *false:*

    a. Two independent clauses in a sentence must be separated by a semicolon or by a comma.

    b. Conjunctive adverbs between independent clauses should have a semicolon or a period preceding them.

    c. A run-on sentence can be corrected by changing one of the independent clauses into a dependent clause.

B. On the line in front of each number write the letter corresponding to the kind of error each sentence contains. If a sentence is correct, write "d" in front of the sentence.

    a. sentence fragment   *c. comma-splice*

    b. run-on sentence   *d. correct*

_____ 6. Pat has a collection of postcards from all over the world, he began his collection when he was in grade school.

_____ 7. The calendar that we use and take for granted has actually been revised or modified several times in past centuries.

_____ 8. Fred sanded the cabinet with fine sandpaper, next he applied several coats of shellac.

_____ 9. After eating a large steak, two baked potatoes with butter and sour cream, extra helpings of spaghetti, a stack of bread, and three large scoops of ice cream, which was a typical meal for him.

_____ 10. Electric typewriters have replaced manual typewriters in most large offices although more expensive to purchase, electric typewriters are more efficient and their users more productive.

_____ 11. Last summer Madeline worked in the complaint department of a large store she learned that a sense of humor is important in such a job.

_____ 12. In his garden Clarence planted potatoes, tomatoes, and corn, he consumed most of the food himself, selling the remainder to his neighbors.

_____ 13. Many radio stations throughout the country continually change their format because they are strongly influenced by fads in musical tastes.

_____ 14. Paperback books, which used to sell for a dollar or less, but which now cost much more.

_____ 15. As the only boy in a family of five children, Earl discovered that there were disadvantages, for example, he recalled that his sisters had to approve of his girl friends.

_____ 16. I decided to keep last semester's textbooks instead of selling them as I usually do.

_____ 17. Hattie complained that the new electric sharpener chewed up her pencils. Leaving only piles of shavings on the floor.

_____ 18. Caroline said that it was impossible to read all of the magazines that she subscribed to, stacks of unread magazines were on the coffee table.

_____ 19. Children all over the world learn nursery rhymes, many of the rhymes have common ideas or themes.

_____ 20. Winston bought a very expensive painting at the auction later he was disappointed to learn that the frame was worth more than the painting.

_____ 21. The skills required for waterskiing are not the same needed for snow skiing, a fact soon discovered by those who have tried both sports.

_____ 22. Although helicopters are usually thought of only in terms of their use in war. They are also used by police rescue teams and news reporters.

_____ 23. Steve's history teacher told the class that Benjamin Franklin invented the rocking chair, Franklin was also the inventor of the lightning rod.

_____ 24. Blue jeans, which used to be worn exclusively for work or very informal situations, can now be seen even in formal occasions.

_____ 25. Food inspectors discovered that horse meat was being sold as beef because of the announcement, sales at many fast-food restaurants declined.

SENTENCE COMBINING WITH ADVERB CLAUSES

Adverb clauses (page 117) act as adverbs in complex sentences: they modify verbs, adjectives, and adverbs. Because they can usually be moved around in a sentence without affecting the meaning, and because they modify words in independent clauses, adverb clauses can often be combined with simple sentences to create longer, smoother complex sentences.

Adverb clauses tell *when, where, why, how,* or *under what conditions* something happens. They usually start with words like *after, although, as soon as, because, before, if, since, unless, until,* and *when.* (See page 117 for additional information about words that introduce adverb clauses.)

Notice how each of the following pairs of sentences is combined into a smoother sentence by the use of an adverb clause:

1. I should have known better. I enrolled in a tap-dancing class.
   (combined) Although I should have known better, *I enrolled in a tap-dancing class.*
2. Tourists visit Niagara Falls. They are awestruck by the grandeur of the scene.
   (combined) When tourists visit Niagara Falls, *they are awestruck by the grandeur of the scene.*
3. *Jeff wants to take a trip to Wales. His parents are Welsh.*
   (combined) *Jeff wants to take a trip to Wales,* because his parents are Welsh.

You should notice two things about adverb clauses. First, they can usually be moved around in the sentence. In sentences 1 and 2, the adverb clause introduces the sentence; in sentence 3, it is at the end of the sentence. The other thing to note is that introductory adverb clauses—those at the beginning of a sentence—are set off by commas. The first two sentences above illustrate this principle.

By changing one of the sentences in each of the following groups to an adverb clause, combine the sentences into smoother complex sentences. Underline the adverb clause, and remember to set off introductory adverb clauses with commas.

1. Truman Capote's first novel was a huge success. He was twenty-four years old.

2. Some athletes ''burn out'' at the height of their careers. They do not derive pleasure from playing any more.

3. Nikki traveled with her husband on his business trips. She used the time to see the local sights.

4. Hank Aaron retired from baseball. He had hit 755 home runs.

5. The President arrived on the platform. The band played ''Hail to the Chief.''

Writing Original Sentences with Adverb Clauses

Write ten original sentences, using adverb clauses. Underline the clauses and remember to set off introductory adverb clauses.

9

Confused Sentences

In previous chapters we have seen how important it is to write sentences that are grammatically correct. To avoid confusion and to make our meaning clear, we must make certain that the subjects and verbs of our sentences agree and that all pronouns refer clearly to their antecedents. But clarity and correctness depend on several other considerations as well. In this chapter we will look at some of the other ways to avoid illogical, inexact, or confused sentences.

MISPLACED AND DANGLING MODIFIERS

Modifiers are words that describe other words in sentences. They may be single words, phrases, or clauses; they may come before the word they modify, or they may follow it. In either case, a modifier should appear *near* the word it modifies, and there should be no confusion about which word it modifies.

A *misplaced modifier* is one that is not close to the word it modifies, and as a result it modifies the wrong word. Sentences with misplaced modifiers are usually confusing and often humorous because of the unintended meaning. But by placing the modifier next to the word it modifies or by rewording the sentence, we can make the meaning of such sentences clear.

Notice the differences in meaning in the following pairs of words; the modifiers are italicized.

(confusing)   *A large bright comet with a tail millions of kilometers long,* Professor LePointe said that Halley's Comet appears every seventy-six years.

(revised)   Professor LePointe said that Halley's Comet, a large bright comet with a tail millions of kilometers long, appears every seventy-six years.

(confusing)   The food was placed in a plastic container *that was not eaten.*

(revised)   The food that was not eaten was placed in a plastic container.

(confusing)   Ms. Becker discussed the high cost of living *with her Congressman.*

(revised)   Ms. Becker discussed with her Congressman the high cost of living.

Exercise 1:

Rewrite any of the following sentences that contain misplaced modifiers. If a sentence is correct, write "C" in front of it.

1. Waving frantically and yelling loudly, the helicopter dipped down low over the marooned climbers.

2. Every St. Patrick's Day my father gave a present to my mother wrapped in green.

3. A pot of coffee was percolating in the kitchen which smelled delicious.

4. Ms. Wright will accept only themes from students in black ink.

5. Sylvester found the wristwatch in his desk drawer that he had lost.

6. The coach only talked to the linemen.

7. Class photographs were sent to graduating seniors that were suitable for framing.

8. Professor Strauss lent me a book for my term paper that was written in German.

9. Sue served drinks to her guests in frosted glasses.

10. I have just finished a novel by Saul Bellow.

A variation of the misplaced modifier is the *squinting modifier,* a modifier that usually appears in the middle of a sentence so that it can modify either the word that precedes it or the one that follows it. As a result, the squinting modifier makes the sentence ambiguous.

The following sentences contain squinting modifiers:

Dean said when his car needed a tune-up he would sell it. (Did he say, *"My car needs a tune-up and therefore I will sell it"?* Or did he say that he would sell the car when it needs a tune-up?)

Clarence decided during the Christmas holiday to get braces on his teeth. (While he was on his Christmas holiday, did Clarence decide to get braces on his teeth? Or did he decide to get braces as soon as he began his holiday?)

As you can see, sentences with squinting modifiers have two possible meanings, and therefore they can be revised in two ways, depending on the meaning. One method is to reword the sentence so that the modifier clearly refers to the intended word:

When his car needed a tune-up, Dean said he would sell it.

Another way to correct a sentence with a squinting modifier is to insert the relative pronoun *that* in the appropriate place:

Dean said that when his car needed a tune-up, he would sell it. **or:** *When his car needed a tune-up, Dean said that he would sell it.*

Applying these methods, we can revise the other sentence:

During the Christmas holiday Clarence decided to get braces on his teeth. **or:** *Clarence decided that he would get braces on his teeth during the Christmas holiday.*

Exercise 2:

Rewrite any of the following sentences that contain squinting modifiers. If a sentence is correct, write "C" in front of it.

1. Vince's mother asked him every week to write her.

2. The master of ceremonies announced during the intermission there would be a surprise for everyone.

3. Mr. Downing said when he completed his fortieth year he would retire.

4. Coach Walker told his team early in the first quarter to try a surprise play.

5. My dentist reminds me regularly to floss my teeth.

6. Anyone who cooks occasionally burns the food.

7. The controller told the pilot when he took off that his right engine was smoking.

8. Drivers who ignore traffic signals often cause accidents.

9. The clothing store where I bought a suit last week burned down.

10. Mr. Royce's story that he told slowly put us all to sleep.

A *dangling modifier* is a modifier that has no word in the sentence for it to modify. It is left "dangling," and as a result it ends up accidentally modifying an unintended word, as in the following example:

> *After reviewing my lecture notes and rereading the summaries of each chapter, the final examination was easier than I had thought.*

According to this sentence, the final examination reviewed the lecture notes and reread the summaries of each chapter. But this is obviously not the meaning intended. To correct this sentence, we must first determine *who* was doing the action. By supplying the missing subject, we can then improve the sentence:

> *After reviewing my lecture notes and rereading the summaries of each chapter, I found that the final examination was easier than I had thought.*
>
> **or:** *After I reviewed my lecture notes and reread the summaries of each chapter, the final examination was easier than I had thought.*

Here are some more sentences with dangling modifiers:

> *Sound asleep, the alarm clock was not heard.*
> *Arriving home after midnight, the house was dark.*
> *Frightened by the noise, the barks of the dog woke us up.*

By supplying subjects and rewording these sentences, we can make their meanings clear:

Sound asleep, I did not hear the alarm clock.

When we arrived home after midnight, the house was dark.

Frightened by the noise, the dog woke us up by its barking.

Tips for Correcting Misplaced and Dangling Modifiers

---

1. Place every modifier close to the word it modifies.
2. If the word meant to be modified is not in the sentence, insert it close to its modifier.
3. Reword or punctuate the sentence so that the intended meaning is clear.

Exercise 3:

Rewrite any of the following sentences that contain dangling modifiers. If a sentence is correct, write "C" in front of it.

1. Standing on the bridge overhead, the water churned and flowed rapidly in its journey south.
2. When working outdoors, cold drinks are brought in an ice chest.
3. Raking leaves in the backyard, a garden snake slithered into a pile of trash.
4. To catch fish, many things must be considered.
5. After talking to my banker, he approved the loan.
6. While in the army overseas, the novel *Ulysses* kept me sane.
7. Pushing the cart through the aisles, the vegetables looked fresh.
8. After putting on my coat, my mother said that I should stay home.
9. Lurching from side to side, Bob's driving made her ill.
10. To stay in shape, running is recommended.

ILLOGICAL COMPARISONS

A comparison is a statement about the relation between two or more things:

> *Sears, Roebuck is larger than any other retailer in the United States.*
> *My father's 1964 Chevrolet runs as well as my new Caprice.*
> *Carl Lewis won more gold medals at the 1984 Olympics than any other athlete.*

When making a comparison, be certain that the things being compared are similar and that your comparison is complete. Omitted words often make the comparison unclear, illogical, or awkward.

(Unclear)   *Tulsa is closer to Oklahoma City than Dallas.*

This sentence is not clear because the comparison is not stated fully enough. Be sure that the comparisons are full enough to be clear.

(Revised)   *Tulsa is closer to Oklahoma City than it is to Dallas.*
(Illogical)   *The population of Mexico City is growing at a faster rate than that of any major city in the world.*

This sentence is illogical because it compares its subject with itself. When comparing members of the same class, use *other* or *any other*.

(Revised)   *The population of Mexico City is growing at a faster rate than that of any* other *major city in the world.*
(Unclear)   *The average hourly wage for a women is lower than a man.*

This sentence is unclear because it compares an hourly wage with a man. Be sure that items being compared are comparable.

(Revised)   *The average hourly wage for a woman is lower than a* man's.

Exercise 4:

Revise any of the following sentences that contain illogical comparisons. If a sentence is correct, write "C" in front of the number.

1. Wanda gave us more salad than LaVerne.

2. The doctor advised Richard that he needed more exercise than us.

3. Although her grades were good, she studied less than any member of the class.

4. Faulkner's writing style is much different from Thomas Wolfe.

5. My uncle boasts that he can drive nails faster than any man.

6. Woodrow Wilson, according to one biographer, had a higher I.Q. than any President of the United States.

7. More books have been written about William Shakespeare than any writer in English literature.

8. The food at The Blue Fox is better than The Albatross.

9. The center on the basketball team had feet bigger than any player on the team.

10. Cadillacs are more popular than any other American luxury car.

CONFUSING ADJECTIVES AND ADVERBS

Adjectives and adverbs are modifiers; they limit or describe other words.

adjective: Moderate *exercise suppresses the appetite.*
  adverb: *The surgeon* carefully *examined the sutures.*

Many adverbs end in *-ly (hurriedly, graciously, angrily)*; some of the most common, however, do not *(here, there, now, when, then, often)*. Furthermore, some words that end in *-ly* are not adverbs *(silly, manly, hilly)*.

Using Adjectives After Linking Verbs

You will recall from Chapter 1 that the most common linking verbs are *be, appear, become, grow, remain, seem,* and the "sense" verbs *(feel, look, smell, sound,* and *taste)*. Words that follow such verbs and refer to the subject are usually *adjectives*—never adverbs. In the following sentences, the adjective (called a *predicate adjective* because it follows the verb and modifies the subject) comes after a linking verb:

Pat's ideas are exciting. (Exciting *modifies* ideas.)

Their wedding reception was expensive. (Expensive *modifies* wedding reception.)

That detergent makes my hands feel rough. (Rough *modifies* hands.)

The rule for deciding whether to use an adjective or an adverb after a verb, therefore, is simple: if the verb shows a condition or a state of being, use an adjective after it. Here are some additional examples that illustrate the rule:

The hamburger smells tantalizing.

Mike's girl friend appeared nervous.

The math final seemed easy.

Marvin looked handsome *in his new suit.*

Most of us would not write or say, ''This soup is warmly,'' or ''She is beautifully.'' In both cases we would instinctively use an adjective rather than an adverb. The choice is not so obvious with ''bad'' and ''well,'' however. Study carefully the use of these words in the sentences below.

(incorrect): *He had some of my homemade soup and now he feels* badly. (Badly *is an adverb following a linking verb; it cannot modify the pronoun* He.)

(correct): *He had some of my homemade soup and now he feels* bad. (Bad *is an adjective modifying* He.)

(incorrect): *I feel* badly *about that. (As in the first example above,* badly *is an adverb and therefore cannot modify the pronoun* I.)

(correct): *I feel* bad *about that. (Bad is an adjective modifying* I.)

(incorrect): *That hat looks very* well *on you. (Looks is a linking verb, and therefore we need an adjective after the verb to modify the noun* hat. Well *is an adverb except when it means ''to be in good health.'')*

(correct): *That hat looks very* good *on you. (Good is an adjective modifying the noun* hat.)

(correct): *Although she has been sick, she looks* well *now. (Well, as noted above, is an adjective when it means ''to be in good health.'' In this sentence it follows the linking verb* looks *and modifies she.)*

Using Adverbs to Modify Verbs

When a verb expresses an *action* by the subject, use an *adverb* after it—not an adjective. Study the following sentences:

(incorrect): *Because Jack was unfamiliar with the city, he drove* careful.
(correct): *Because Jack was unfamiliar with the city, he drove* carefully.
(incorrect): *Lorraine spoke very* quiet *of her many accomplishments.*
(correct): *Lorraine spoke very* quietly *of her many accomplishments.*
(incorrect): *Sharon picked up the expensive glass* delicate.
(correct): *Sharon picked up the expensive glass* delicately.

Verbs that sometimes show condition or state of being in one sentence but an action by the subject in another sentence can be troublesome:

The dog smelled the meat carefully. (Smelled *is an* action *verb.)*
The meat smelled rotten. (Smelled *is a* linking *verb.)*

The alarm sounded suddenly. (Sounded *is an* action *verb.)*
His cries sounded pitiful. (Sounded *is a* linking *verb.)*

Arlene appeared tired. (Appeared *is a* linking *verb.*)
Arlene appeared abruptly. (Appeared *is an* action *verb.*)

Tips for Choosing Adverbs or Adjectives

The choice of an adverb or an adjective depends on the kind of verb in the sentence:
1. If the verb is *linking* and you want to describe the subject, an *adjective* is correct.
2. If you want to modify a verb that shows *action,* an *adverb* is correct.

Exercise 5:

Write the letter of the correct word on the line preceding the sentence.

_____ 1. Despite his nervousness, Neil performed (a. *well,*   b. *good)* on the trampoline.

_____ 2. In geometry, the theorems and proofs lead (a. *logical,*   b. *logically)* to the answers.

_____ 3. Because I wound the clock too (a. *tight,*   b. *tightly),* it gained ten minutes during the night.

_____ 4. Although the peanut butter tasted (a. *delicious,*   b. *deliciously),* I realized that I did not need the calories.

_____ 5. Claire answered the telephone (a. *hastily,*   b. *hasty)* when it rang during lunch.

_____ 6. Her answers were (a. *hastily,*   b. *hasty)* rather than deliberate.

_____ 7. After four consecutive days of rain, the sun felt (a. *good,*   b. *well).*

_____ 8. The pictures and furniture in Dale's room match his personality (a. *perfect,*   b. *perfectly).*

_____ 9. Although Christine appeared (a. *good,*   b. *well)* this morning, she became ill after lunch and went home.

_____ 10. The streets of the city remained (a. *peaceful,*   b. *peacefully)* after the riot.

PARALLEL STRUCTURE

When writing about items in a series, be sure that you present each item in the same grammatical form. In other words, each item should be an adjective or a prepositional phrase or an infinitive, and so on. When all items in a series are in the same grammatical form, the sentence or passage is said to have *parallel structure.*

Notice the use of parallel structure in the following sentences:

His duties are to order supplies, to keep an inventory, *and* to maintain records of returns. *(three infinitives)*

Margaret's work is accurate *and* neat. *(two adjectives)*

The dog escaped from its cage, dashed into the street, *and* ignored the calls of its master. *(three verbs)*

Paul quit smoking because it was an expensive habit *and* because his wife had quit. *(two dependent clauses)*

Parallel structure is a writing technique worth acquiring because it makes sentences smoother and shows the connection between ideas. For these reasons, professional writers and public speakers often make use of parallel structure. Study carefully the following excerpt from Abraham Lincoln's second inaugural address. It has been arranged so that the parallelism can easily be seen.

With malice toward none,
with charity for all,
with firmness in the right as God gives us to see the right,
    let us strive on
        to finish the work we are in,
        to bind up the nation's wounds,
        to care for him who shall have born the battle
          and for his widow and his orphan,
        to do all which may achieve and cherish
          a just and lasting peace
            among ourselves
            and
          with all nations.

In your own writing, parallelism can ''bind up'' a sentence, making its parts and meaning much easier to grasp. Notice the difference between the following pairs of sentences:

(faulty)   *Professor Dwyer's lectures are* interesting *and a* challenge. (adjective and noun)

(parallel) *Professor Dwyer's lectures are* interesting *and* challenging. (two adjectives)

(faulty)   *Everyone was having a good time. Some* people were dancing, others were talking, *and* television was watched by a few. (Two clauses in the active voice and one clause in the passive voice) (parallel) *Everyone was having a good time. Some* people were dancing, others were talking, *and* a few were watching television. (Three clauses in the active voice)

(faulty) *During his vacation, Norman wants* to paint his house, visit his family in Kansas, catch up on his reading, *and also* working in his garden. (three infinitives and a gerund)

(parallel) *During his vacation, Norman wants* to paint his house, visit his family in Kansas, catch up on his reading, *and* work in his garden. (four infinitives)

Correlative Conjunctions

You can also achieve effective parallel construction by using *correlative conjunctions.* As mentioned in Chapter 1, correlatives are connectives used in pairs, and therefore they are handy tools for linking similar grammatical patterns with ideas of similar importance. The most common correlatives are *either/or, neither/nor, not only/but also,* and *both/and.*

Here are some examples of correlative conjunctions used to achieve parallel structure:

Sheila is proficient not only *on the clarinet* but also *on the saxophone.*

Neither *the musicians* nor *the producers could have predicted the success of rock music on television.*

The President's remarks were addressed both *to Congress* and *to the American people.*

When using correlative conjunctions, be sure to place them as closely as possible to the words they join.

(incorrect) *She* neither *wanted our advice* nor our help.
(correct) *She wanted* neither *our advice* nor *our help.*
(incorrect) *Ellen will be flying* both *to Minneapolis and Chicago.*
(correct) *Ellen will be flying to* both *Minneapolis and Chicago.*
(incorrect) *Richard would* neither *apologize* nor *would he admit that he was wrong.*
(correct) *Richard would* neither *apologize* nor *admit that he was wrong.*

Exercise 6:

Rewrite any of the following sentences that contain faulty parallelism. If the sentence is correct, write ''C'' before the number.

1. Teresa speaks not only English but Spanish also.

2. Either I must reduce my expenses or get a part-time job.

3. Our guide told us that we should see the Tower of London, the British Museum, and that we should also visit Stonehenge.

4. The novels of Charles Dickens are loved because he has unforgettable characters, his ability to tell a good story, and we laugh and cry.

5. Dolly's mother is not only funny but also absentminded.

6. I neither received thanks nor appreciation for my suggestions.

7. In Robert's new job he will interview applicants, supervise noncertificated employees, and he will also be responsible for evaluating probationary employees.

8. The business venture left him impoverished, suspicious, and an angry man.

9. Writing the term paper was time-consuming, while also being a chance to learn about entomology.

10. According to Zsa Zsa Gabor, it is better to be rich than being poor.

9

Review Exericse

On the line in front of each number write the letter corresponding to the kind of error each sentence contains.

> a. misplaced or dangling modifier
>
> b. illogical or incomplete comparison
>
> c. adjective or adverb used incorrectly
>
> d. faulty parallel structure

_____ 1. On the weekends Carl spends most of his time working at the laundry, studying for his classes, and sometimes he watches television.

_____ 2. Muriel argued that the cartoons in *Mad* are funnier than the *New Yorker* magazine.

_____ 3. After scraping the old paint and applying putty to the exposed nail holes, the house was ready to be trimmed in its new colors.

_____ 4. Having lived on an isolated farm all of her life, downtown Philadelphia was somewhat confusing at first.

_____ 5. When the hotel clerk asked for my room number, I felt very foolishly when I could not remember it.

_____ 6. By the funny taste of the salad I realized I either used too much garlic or too many herbs.

_____ 7. The car salesperson claimed that this year's models were safer to drive, cheaper to maintain, and use less gas.

_____ 8. The fumes from the cleaning fluid smelled badly, giving me a headache.

_____ 9. Celebrating her fiftieth birthday, a surprise party was given.

_____ 10. Although Ms. Zimmer has written two cookbooks, she always speaks very modest of her own cooking.

_____ 11. Tyler felt badly about not being able to meet his friends after work.

_____ 12. Emil thought that all you had to do to impress your friends was to wear the latest clothes, drive an expensive car, and also you should flash a roll of big bills.

_____ 13. Although Janet's writing is very precise and exact, she speaks careless and without regard to correct usage.

_____ 14. Mr. Darrow looked suspicious at me when he noticed that the bag of gum drops had been opened.

_____ 15. Breaking into the sales manager's office during the night, the keys for a new sports car were stolen.

_____ 16. Slamming on the brakes and blowing the horn, the pedestrian darted from the path of the car.

_____ 17. While still a child, Nelson Rockefeller's parents established a trust fund for him.

_____ 18. To understand the game of cricket, watching the game with someone who has played it would be helpful.

_____ 19. The designer told Carol that pastel shades look very well on her.

_____ 20. By carefully reading the directions, the bicycle was assembled.

_____ 21. While kicking the ball for his second goal of the night, his ankle was twisted.

_____ 22. Gail's tips as a waitress were more than the other waitresses.

_____ 23. The hunter moved very cautious through the underbrush to avoid making a sound.

_____ 24. She looked terribly as a result of her experiences on the trip.

_____ 25. I dusted the shelves very careful, trying to avoid breaking any of the valuable glasses and dishes.

SENTENCE COMBINING WITH NOUN CLAUSES

Noun clauses (page 122) function as subjects, objects, and subject complements. When an independent clause can be converted into a dependent clause and used as the subject, object, or complement of another sentence, the result is usually a smoother sentence.

Notice how the following pairs of short sentences can be combined by changing one of the sentences to a noun clause and combining it with the other sentence:

1. *The ethics committee prepared its report. It stated that the candidate had not broken the law.*
(combined)   *The ethics committee's report stated* that the candidate had not broken the law.
2. *The cause of the explosion is unknown. It is a mystery to the authorities.*
(combined)   What caused the explosion *is a mystery to the authorities.*
3. *Dwight told me a secret. He is going to get married.*
(combined)   *Dwight told me* that he is going to get married.

Combine the following sets of sentences by using noun clauses. Underline the noun clause in your sentence.

1. Last night I had a dream. I was stranded on an island with my calculus textbook.

2. I remember now. You owe me five dollars.

3. The defendant suddenly confessed. He had forged the checks.

4. My father had a saying. No one ever got rich on a salary alone.

5. Many chess grandmasters are Russian. This is because of the popularity of the game in Russia.

Writing Original Sentences with Noun Clauses

Write ten original sentences, using noun clauses. Underline the noun clauses.

10

Punctuation

When we speak, we make our meaning clear with more than just words. We pause at certain times, raise our voices for emphasis, and use various body movements. When we write, we use punctuation marks for the same purpose: to make our meaning intelligible to the reader. Every mark of punctuation carries some meaning and gives hints about how to read written English.

Careless punctuation can change meaning and confuse or even mislead the reader. Occasionally, the cost may be dramatic, as in a recently publicized Florida case in which nonprofit organizations lost two million dollars because a comma changed the meaning of a sentence and thereby rendered them ineligible for sales tax exemptions. Learning to punctuate correctly is not hard. It does, however, require a little patience. In this chapter we will look at the most common situations in written English that require punctuation.

END PUNCTUATION

The Period

Use the period at the end of a declarative sentence, an indirect question, or a mild command.

Declarative sentence:	*In 1831, Nat Turner led a short but bloody slave revolt in Virginia.*
Indirect question:	*She asked us if we wanted to go.*
Mild command:	*Please return these books to the library.*

Use a period after most abbreviations.

A.D. a.m. Ms. Mr. oz. Nov. M.A.

When an abbreviation ends a sentence, only one period is needed.

A lecture on interdigitation will be given by Leonard Zellman, Ph.D.

Periods do not usually follow acronyms and abbreviations of well-known organizations and governmental agencies.

IBM NBC AFL NOW UNESCO USFL NATO

The Question Mark

Use a question mark after a direct question.

On which side of a tree does the moss always grow?

Do *not* use a question mark after an indirect question.

He asked me on which side of a tree the moss always grows.

Use a question mark to indicate uncertainty about the accuracy of a word, a phrase, or a date.

The Greek philosopher Plato (427?–347 B.C.) was a disciple of Socrates.

The Exclamation Point

Use an exclamation point after a strong interjection or an expression of very strong feeling.

No! It can't be true!
Hurry! We'll be late!

Be careful not to overdo the exclamation point. When overused, it creates an almost hysterical tone in writing. Use a comma or a period instead of an exclamation point after a mild interjection.

No, I don't think I want to.

Exercise 1:

Supply a period, question mark, or exclamation point where needed. If there is no room in the sentence, insert a caret (∧) below the line and write the appropriate punctuation above the line.

1. I would like to ask Prof Hurtik whether I could have an appointment for ten am tomorrow

2. After getting his degree from St Louis University, Bernie worked for the FBI office in Springfield

3. Now that I have a new watch, no one asks me what time it is

4. Ed refuses to tell us why he came home so late

5. If my contact lenses blur my vision, does it mean they are the wrong size

6. Wow What a catch Winslow made

7. Dr Teresa O'Reilly is chief surgeon at St John's Hospital on Lunday Ave

8. The favorite expression of Harry Caray, the Chicago Cubs' announcer, is ''Holy Cow''

9. The Rev George W Smith gave the benediction at the graduation ceremony

10. Please pick me up at eight o'clock

11. My cynical Uncle Bud wants to know whether there is life after birth

12. Do you know the real title of the painting of the Mona Lisa

13. Many psychologists and educators wonder why girls usually get lower scores than boys on math tests

14. Help I'm drowning in homework

15. Can you tell me where the Helmut Dantine Fan Club is meeting

INTERNAL PUNCTUATION

The Comma

The comma is the punctuation mark most frequently used inside the sentence. It also offers the widest range of individual choice. As a result, many writers are uncertain concerning its proper use, and they sprinkle commas indiscriminately through their sentences. Do not use a comma unless you have a definite reason for doing so. The rules below will help you avoid cluttering your sentences with unnecessary commas while at the same time making certain you use commas to make your meaning clear.

Use a comma to separate independent clauses joined by a coordinating conjunction *(and, but, for, nor, or, so, yet)*.

> *Roy was disappointed at the results of the election*, but *his face concealed his feelings.*
>
> *Marcia took a course in graphics last semester*, and *now she works for a photographer.*
>
> *I could not remember Phil's address*, nor *could I recall his telephone number.*

NOTE: *Do* not *use a comma between two independent clauses that are not joined by a coordinating conjunction. This error creates a* comma-splice *(see Chapter 8). Use a semicolon or start a new sentence.*

When one or both independent clauses in a compound sentence are short, you may omit the commas before the conjunction.

> *I read and Steve watched television.*
>
> *I'm tired but I'm ready.*

Do not use a comma before a coordinating conjunction linking two words, phrases, or dependent clauses.

(incorrect)   *Shakespeare wrote plays, and acted in the London theater. (The conjunction* and *does not join two independent clauses.)*

(correct)   *Shakespeare wrote plays and acted in the London theater.*

(incorrect)	*Many sailors become proficient in navigation, but neglect the problem of anchoring.*
(correct)	*Many sailors become proficient in navigation but neglect the problem of anchoring.*

Use a comma to separate an introductory dependent clause from the main part of the sentence.

Although David was afraid of the water, *he overcame his fear and learned to swim.*

When we visited Chicago last summer, *we went to a baseball game at Wrigley Field.*

Use a comma after a long introductory prepositional phrase.

After an arduous trek over snowcapped mountains and scorched desert floors, *the Mormons finally reached Utah.*

In preparing your annual report to the board of directors, *be sure to include predictions for next year's sales.*

Use a comma to set off an introductory participial phrase.

Pleased by the initial reaction from the voters, *the Democratic candidate stepped up his attack on his opponent.*

Remembering the promise made to his parents, *Jeff carefully kept a record of his purchases and entered each payment in his checkbook.*

Do not put a comma after participial phrases that are actually the subject of the sentence.

(incorrect)	*Watering his lawn, was Mr. Dawson's only exercise.*
(correct)	*Watering his lawn was Mr. Dawson's only exercise.*
(incorrect)	*Reading about Oliver Cromwell's treatment of the Irish, made me more aware of the background behind the troubles in Ulster today.*
(correct)	*Reading about Oliver Cromwell's treatment of the Irish made me more aware of the background behind the troubles in Ulster today.*

Use a comma to set off an introductory infinitive phrase unless the phrase is the subject of the sentence.

To win the jackpot in Las Vegas, you must overcome tremendous odds.

But: *To win the jackpot in Las Vegas was his dream.*
To impress his future in-laws, Bill wore a suit and tie.

But: *To impress his future in-laws might have been possible if Bill had worn a suit and tie.*

Use a comma after an introductory request or command.

Look, *we've been through all of this before.*

Remember, *tomorrow is the deadline for filing your tax return.*

Use a comma to separate three or more items in a series unless all of the items are joined by *and* or *or.*

The gymnasium was small, crowded, and stuffy.

But: *The gymnasium was small and crowded and stuffy.*

Rick made some sandwiches, Jo Ann brought her guitar, and I furnished the soft drinks.

John looked for the receipt in the drawer, under the bed, behind the sofa, and in his wallet.

Use a comma to separate interrupting elements (words, phrases and clauses) when they break the flow of a sentence.

It is a fact, isn't it, *that the spleen filters the blood?*

I will hold your mail for you or, if you prefer, *forward it to your hotel.*

We could use, if possible, *six more cartons of eggs.*

Other interrupting elements (also called *parenthetical elements* or *transitional expressions)* include the following: *as a matter of fact, at any rate, for instance, nevertheless, of course, therefore, in my opinion,* and *on the other hand.* These and similar phrases are usually set off by commas when they appear in a sentence.

There are three good reasons, I believe, *for changing my major.*

The Rams and the Jets, for example, *have acquired new quarterbacks.*

Newark, on the other hand, *is an industrial city.*

Use a comma to set off direct address and words like *please, yes,* and *no.*

Will you help me, please?

No, *I don't think that the Colts will win tomorrow.*

You should take this medicine, Art, *because it is good for you.*

Exercise 2:

Add commas to the following sentences wherever needed. If no comma is needed in a sentence, place a "C" in front of it.

1. C. S. Lewis was a well-known scholar but he was also the author of several novels for young people.

2. Among my more mentionable fantasies are working as the captain in a French restaurant serving as a guide on a riverboat and playing the bass with *The Grateful Dead.*

3. Warren rides his bicycle six miles to work for the exercise but at lunch he eats six doughnuts filled with jelly and then drinks a chocolate malt.

4. If it were up to me Cheryl I'd hire you immediately.

5. Realizing that I was not impressing anyone with my rendition of "Casey at the Bat" I sat down convinced they did not appreciate great literature.

6. The Yankees are favored of course to win the pennant.

7. Rosemary thyme basil and tarragon are my favorite herbs when I make soup.

8. The state of California in fact is one of the major agricultural states in the country.

9. Driving through the countryside in southern Italy we often noticed the remains of ancient Roman aquaducts many still in use.

10. Yes it is possible but I doubt it don't you?

11. Stephen King's novels are gripping and the movie versions are equally suspenseful.

12. Mel majored in economics during his freshman year but later switched to political science much to his father's regret.

13. The Big Ten conference includes Missouri Illinois Iowa Michigan and Wisconsin.

14. When it became obvious that we would win easily the coach sent in the second team.

15. To tell the truth I bought the fish at a market on the way back from the lake Dad.

Additional Uses of the Comma

Use a comma to set off modifiers that are not essential to the sense of the sentence. *Nonessential (or nonrestrictive)* modifiers are those that add information to the sentence, but they modify things or persons already clearly identified in the sentence.

Nonessential clauses are set off by commas (see Chapter 7).

> *My wife*, who was born in St. Louis, *is the oldest of five children. (The adjective clause* who was born in St. Louis *is not essential to the identity of the subject* wife, *nor is it required for the central meaning of the sentence. Therefore, it is nonessential and is set off by commas.)*

But: *Anyone who was born in St. Louis is eligible to apply for the scholarship. (The adjective clause* who was born in St. Louis *is essential to the meaning of the sentence. Not everyone is eligible to apply for the scholarship—just those born in St. Louis. The clause is therefore essential and is not set off by commas.)*

Nonessential appositives are set off by commas. Most appositives are nonessential and require commas.

> *Alexander Hamilton*, the first Secretary of the Treasury of the United States, *was killed in a duel. (The fact that Alexander Hamilton was the first Secretary of the Treasury gives further information about the subject, but it is not essential to the meaning of the sentence. Therefore, the appositive is set off with commas.)*
>
> *Ms. Blanchard*, my chemistry professor, *was educated at Oxford University. (Like the preceding appositive,* my chemistry professor *gives additional but nonessential information about the subject and is therefore set off with commas.)*

Some appositives are restrictive or essential—that is, they are needed in the sentence to identify the element they rename. In such cases they are not set off with commas.

> *The poet Milton worked for the Puritan government. (Which poet worked for the Puritan government? We would not know, unless the appositive* Milton *were included. Therefore, the appositive is essential and commas are not used.)*

Use a comma to set off coordinate adjectives. Adjectives are coordinate if *and* can be placed between them. They describe different qualities of the same noun and may be separated by a comma rather than *and*.

> *a long, boring movie (a long* and *boring movie)*

an expensive, rare gem (an expensive and rare gem)

Some adjectives are not coordinate, and therefore no commas are used to separate them.

dirty blue jeans

a retired staff sergeant

an exciting street scene

Notice that you would not write:

dirty and blue jeans

a retired and staff sergeant

an exciting and street scene

Adjectives usually precede the word they describe; when they *follow* the word they describe, they are set off with commas.

(usual order)   *The loud and unruly crowd stormed the castle gates.*
(inverted order)   *The crowd, loud and unruly, stormed the castle gates.*

Exercise 3:

Add commas to the following sentences wherever needed. If a sentence does not need a comma, write "C" in front of it.

1. Despite her age Marilyn enrolled in a gymnastics class practiced diligently and mastered several intricate maneuvers on the parallel bars coming in third in the state contest the first grandmother to do so.

2. Basketball players who are short rarely play center on the team.

3. Recorded by Joan Baez fifteen years ago the album a two-record set continues to sell thousands of copies annually.

4. One of the things that we do not intend to do in Ireland next summer is kiss the Blarney Stone.

5. The little red schoolhouse a symbol in American education exists only in a few isolated rural communities according to a recent survey.

6. Charles Lindbergh who was one of America's genuine heroes was a painfully shy man.

7. The novel that I like best is James Joyce's *Ulysses* which takes place in Dublin.

8. The boys exhausted frightened and cold managed a feeble cheer when they saw the circling plane.

9. Anyone who purchases a ticket in the statewide lottery should realize that the chances of winning are very slight.

10. The large white house at the end of this street belongs to Professor March who plays chess raises orchids and makes violins as hobbies.

More Uses of the Comma

Use a comma to set off contrasted elements.

> *Her birthday is in July, not August.*
> *Jeff always gets a hotel room downtown, never in the suburbs.*

Use a comma to set off quoted material.

> *Hope announced proudly, "I've been promoted to office manager."*
> *"My wife just gave birth to twins," Dennis said.*

Use commas to set off the year in complete dates.

> *November 22, 1963, is a day that everyone living at the time will always remember.*
> *The September 10, 1984, issue of* Time *featured an article on the new science of conception.*

When only the month and year are given, the comma is optional.

(correct)   *The first commercial telecast took place in April 1939.*
(correct)   *The first commerical telecast took place in April, 1939.*

Use a comma to separate the elements in an address.

> *United Nations Plaza, Riverside Drive, New York, New York*

Within a sentence, place a comma after the final element in an address.

> *His office at the United Nations Plaza on Riverside Drive, New York, is his headquarters.*

Abbreviations standing for academic degrees are set off by commas on both sides.

> *Louis L. Dehner, Ph.D., will address the graduating class.*
> *A plaque recognizing his contributions to the community was given to William G. Bolton, M.D.* (Notice that only one period is necessary at the end of a sentence.)

Use a comma to prevent misreading. In some sentences it is necessary to use a comma even though no rule requires one.

(confusing) *As you know nothing happened at the meeting.*
  (clear) *As you know, nothing happened at the meeting.*
(confusing) *Shortly after he quit his job and moved to Wisconsin.*
  (clear) *Shortly after, he quit his job and moved to Wisconsin.*
(confusing) *While we ate the dog continued to bark.*
  (clear) *While we ate, the dog continued to bark.*

Exercise 4:

Add commas where necessary in the following sentences. If a sentence does not need a comma, write "C" in front of it.

1. If you fail a test you should examine your study techniques.

2. "Either marry me" said Sam "or lend me bus fare back to Hollywood so that I can pursue my career."

3. We left her knowing that we would never return.

4. The insurance company mailed the check to Merrit V. Osborn M.D. whose office is at 4612 Atlantic Boulevard Daytona Beach Florida 32015.

5. On June 11 1970 in Washington D.C. Anna Mae Hays and Elizabeth P. Hoisington both WACS were named the first women generals in the entire history of the United States Army.

6. My friend Tony who thinks of himself as God's gift to women loves to quote George Bernard Shaw who said "The fickleness of women I love is equaled only by the infernal constancy of the women who love me."

7. Although angry Phil continued to play.

8. My summer address will be 1661 Heber Court Broxley Surrey England.

9. Tom asked "Does the comma go inside the closing quotation marks?"

10. Albert Einstein was born on March 14 1879 in Wurttemberg West Germany and died on April 18 1955 in Princeton New Jersey where he had lived for twenty years.

Misusing Commas

When in doubt, many writers are tempted to add commas to their sentences. Too many commas, however, can slow down the thought or confuse the meaning. Here are some of the frequent situations that might tempt you to use the comma.

1. Do not use a comma after the last item in a series of adjectives preceding the noun.

(incorrect)   *She was a dedicated, imaginative, creative, painter.*
(correct)   *She was a dedicated, imaginative, creative painter.*

2. Do not use a comma to separate the subject from its verb.

(incorrect)   *A good night's rest, is the best preparation for a test.*
(correct)   *A good night's rest is the best preparation for a test.*

3. Do not use a comma between two words joined by a coordinating conjunction.

(incorrect)   *Bruce grows tomatoes, and lettuce in his garden.*
(correct)   *Bruce grows tomatoes and lettuce in his garden.*

4. Do not separate a verb from a *that* clause.

(incorrect)   *The Surgeon General has determined, that cigarette smoking is dangerous to your health.*
(correct)   *The Surgeon General has determined that cigarette smoking is dangerous to your health.*

5. Do not use a comma to separate independent clauses unless the comma is followed by a coordinate conjunction (see Chapter 8 for comma-splices).

(incorrect)   *The blaze began in the arid Bull Mountains, it destroyed much of the nearby town of Roundup.*
(correct)   *The blaze began in the arid Bull Mountains, and it destroyed much of the nearby town of Roundup.*

Exercise 5:

Delete or add commas in the following sentences. If a sentence is punctuated correctly, write "C" in front of it.

1. It has been proven, that television shows emphasizing violence, have a harmful effect on their young viewers.

2. A tall, handsome, American man elbowed his way to the head of the line, and demanded to see the ambassador.

© 1986 Scott, Foresman and Company

3. The divers tried to lift the hull to the surface but their efforts failed.

4. Eve gave her husband a blowtorch, a chainsaw, a shotgun, and a new fry-ing pan, for Christmas.

5. When Allen returned to the parking lot he discovered that he had left his car's headlights on and that the battery, was dead.

6. The citizens' group announced, that it was going to investigate the books, and magazines in the local library.

7. Abortion has become a topic of political debate within recent years.

8. Thomas A. Edison was a brilliant, imaginative, resourceful, inventor, who patented hundreds of inventions.

9. Intelligence tests, are not the only measurements of a person's abilities.

10. The Cuban missile crisis was a test of John F. Kennedy's ability, to handle a crisis.

The Semicolon

Use a semicolon to separate two related independent clauses when there is no coordinating conjunction to join them.

> *The law is clear; the question is whether it is enforceable.*
>
> *Competition for admittance to medical school is intense; only about one applicant in twenty is admitted.*

If you use a comma instead of a semicolon for an omitted conjunction, you will create a comma-splice (see Chapter 8 and page 165 in this chapter). There is an exception to this rule in the case of compound sentences in which the clauses are very short:

> *I came, I saw, I conquered.*

Use a semicolon to separate independent clauses joined by a *conjunctive adverb*. Conjunctive adverbs are words like the following: *however, moreover, therefore, furthermore, nevertheless, nonetheless, consequently, otherwise, besides, and hence* (see Chapter 8).

Conjunctive adverbs are not conjunctions, and therefore they require more than a comma before them. When they come at the beginning of an indepen-dent clause, a semicolon or period should precede them. If they are not pre-ceded by a semicolon or period, the result is a comma-splice.

(comma-splice)   *Ford Motors is building a plant in Mexico, moreover, it is also holding talks with Korean manufacturers.*

(correct) *Ford Motors is building a plant in Mexico; moreover, it is also holding talks with Korean manufacturers.*

(comma-splice) *Ray and his wife moved from Buffalo several years ago, however, they still follow the Buffalo Bills and subscribe to a Buffalo newspaper.*

(correct) *Ray and his wife moved from Buffalo several years ago; however, they still follow the Buffalo Bills and subscribe to a Buffalo newspaper.*

Use a semicolon to separate items in a series if the items contain commas.

> *Attending the sales meeting were Marino Garcia, the sales manager; Jim Gleeson, vice president; Lisa Crow, advertising manager; and John Jacobs, secretary-treasurer.*

> *Candidates for the Most Inspiring Player of the Year Award were Bruce Stoecker, fullback; Don Sawyer, tight end; Dick Farley, quarterback; and Joe Reeves, fullback.*

Exercise 6:

Add a semicolon or comma where needed in the following sentences and delete any unnecessary punctuation. If a sentence is punctuated correctly, write "C" in front of it.

1. Everyone criticizes junk food, however, even its harshest critics can't deny its appeal.

2. Because Mr. Price is often grumpy in the morning, we put a cup of black coffee on his desk before class.

3. Charlene decided to leave before dinner for the roads were becoming icy.

4. I have to find a job this semester or I will have to get a loan for tuition.

5. Dolphins are reputed to have high intelligence some scientists have attempted to communicate with them.

6. The advertising agency selected nine cities as trial markets for the new product: Minneapolis, Rochester, and St. Paul in Minnesota, Syracuse, Scarsdale, and Buffalo in New York, and Durham, Charlotte, and Raleigh in North Carolina.

7. The movie was boring, I should have left.

8. Kahn speaks English at school, at home, however, he speaks Vietnamese.

9. The biggest roller rink in town closed permanently last week, the owners plan to lease the building to a church.

10. Peggy found an apartment that she liked, however, the owner wanted a two-month deposit in advance.

The Colon

The colon can be thought of as an equal sign; it tells the reader that what follows it is equivalent to what precedes it. The most common use of the colon is to introduce a list of items after an independent clause:

The trade minister stated that his nation offered potential investors several advantages: a good climate, a sound economy, and a reasonable wage structure.

Yiddish is made up chiefly of words from four languages: Russian, German, Polish, and Hebrew.

The colon is also used to introduce a word or phrase that renames or explains an earlier idea in the sentence:

The president of the union announced that he had only one goal for the forthcoming year: a sizeable wage increase.

The colon can be used between two complete thoughts when the second explains the first:

It was becoming painfully obvious to him: he was being ignored.

A less frequent use of the colon is after a list of items preceding an independent clause:

Cuba, Brazil, and Australia: these are the largest producers of cane sugar.

Do *not* place a colon between a verb and its objects or complements, or between a preposition and its objects.

(incorrect) *Her favorite science-fiction writers are: Robert Heinlein, Isaac Asimov, and Harlan Ellison.*

(incorrect) *While in Windsor, Ontario, we saw: the Hiram Walker Brewery, Willistead Manor, and several fine examples of the city's turn-of-the-century architecture.*

(incorrect) *Charlie Chaplin was easily recognized by: his black mustache, his walk, and his black hat.*

A colon can be used to introduce a quotation that does not form part of a clause or phrase in the rest of the sentence:

As Neil Armstrong put his foot on the surface of the moon, he made a statement that has become famous: "That's one small step for a man, one giant leap for mankind."

Other uses of the colon are after salutations in business letters and between hours and minutes when referring to time:

Dear Professor Baker:

4:05 p.m.

Exercise 7:

Insert a colon where needed in the following sentences, and delete any colons that are unnecessary or incorrect.

1. When I was a teenager, I had a goal I wanted to own a 1955 Cadillac.

2. In a recent survey asking readers to name ten books they would take with them on a long trip, two works were overwhelming favorites the Bible and the plays of Shakespeare.

3. As a hardware store clerk I learned about: paint, varnish, shellac, thinner, stains, and brushes.

4. The chief ingredients for a successful party are the following good food, loud music, and interesting guests.

5. Rudy faced a dilemma whether to watch Monday Night Football or wash his dog.

6. Only one obstacle kept Rick from writing his novel lack of talent.

7. My mother used to say: that the world is divided into two groups those who are Irish and those who wish they were.

8. There are three things I can't stand eggplant, bores, and bow ties.

9. There are three ways to get to Carnegie Hall practice, practice, practice.

10. Professor Lisano gave a lecture on the novel he regards as the greatest to emerge from South America *One Hundred Years of Solitude,* by Gabriel Garcia Marquez.

Parentheses

Use parentheses to enclose unimportant information or comments that are not an essential part of the passage. In this respect parentheses are like commas; the difference is that they evoke the reader's attention more than commas.

Mapmakers use a system of meridians of longitude (from the Latin longus, *"long") and parallels of latitude (from* latus, *"wide").*

Zane Grey (who started out as a dentist) is one of the most popular novelists of the American West.

Whitman's Leaves of Grass *(published in 1855) was greeted with hostility.*

Dates that accompany an event or a person's name are enclosed in parentheses.

The Teapot Dome scandal (1929) involved several figures in the cabinet of President Harding.

Ernest Hemingway (1898–1961) was the author of a little-known stage play.

NOTE: *Never insert a comma, a semicolon, a colon, or a dash before an opening parenthesis.*

(incorrect)   *Hal David, (Burt Bacharach's collaborator) wrote the lyrics to "Alfie."*

Dashes

The dash is a forceful punctuation mark, and it must be used carefully. It often takes the place of the comma, the semicolon, the colon, or parentheses in a sentence in order to separate emphatically words or groups of words. The difference between the dash and these other marks is that it focuses attention on the items being separated.

Use a dash to mark an abrupt change in the thought or structure of a sentence:

I wonder if we should—oh, let's take care of it later.

Use a dash to make parenthetical or explanatory matter more prominent:

George Halas—one of the founders of the National Football League—was known as "Papa Bear."

The family's belongings—their clothing, furniture, stereo set, and other possessions—were stolen during their weekend absence.

Use a dash to set off single words that require emphasis:

Paul thinks about only one thing—money.

Use a dash to set off an appositive or an introductory series:

Only one northern industrial state—Illinois—has not ratified the Equal Rights Amendment.

NOTE: *The use of dashes in this sentence emphasizes the appositive* Illinois; *parentheses would also be correct, but they would not present the same emphasis.*

Leonardo da Vinci, William the Conqueror, Alexander Hamilton, and Richard Wagner—they were all illegitimate children.

NOTE: *A colon would also be correct in this sentence after* Richard Wagner.

Exercise 8:

Depending on the desired emphasis, insert parentheses or dashes in the following sentences.

1. Leif Ericson not Christopher Columbus was the first European to set foot on the shores of North America, according to my Swedish friends.

2. Research into R.E.M. Rapid Eye Movement suggests that there is a relationship between the rate of blinking and the kinds of dreams one has.

3. I intend to lose I really mean this ten pounds in the next two weeks.

4. Many baseball fans in large cities for example, Memphis, Syracuse, Miami, and Portland are clamoring for major-league teams.

5. Expressive gestures biological gestures of the kind we share with other animals include shouting, smiling, and grimacing.

6. I read an article in the *Times* or maybe it was the *News-Dispatch* describing the recent tornado in southern Illinois.

7. Stubby my pet dog that I told you about loves light beer.

8. Law, navigation, medicine, science, war, politics Shakespeare wrote with knowledge about these and other topics in his plays.

9. The dessert which consisted of strawberries soaked in brandy and dipped in chocolate climaxed the feast.

10. Sales of his novel over sixty thousand in the last two years have exceeded the publisher's expectations.

Quotation Marks

Quotation marks have three main functions: to indicate the exact words of a speaker, to call attention to words used in an unusual sense or in definitions, and to enclose the title of certain kinds of literary and artistic works. In every case, be sure that you use them in pairs; a common mistake is to omit the last set of quotation marks.

FOR DIRECT QUOTATIONS Use quotation marks around the exact words of a speaker.

Grandpa announced, "It's time to take my nap."

"We do," the nervous bridegroom whispered.

Notice that a comma precedes quotation marks in a direct quotation and that the first word of the quotation is capitalized. Do not use quotation marks for indirect quotations.

Grandpa announced that it was time to take his nap.

Always place commas and periods *inside* the end quotation marks.

"If you wait a few minutes," she said, "we will walk to the corner with you."

When the quotation is a question or exclamation, place the question mark or exclamation point *inside* the quotation marks.

She asked with a smile, "Who left this on my desk?"

"That music is too loud!" my father shouted.

When the question mark or exclamation point applies to the entire sentence and not just to the quotation, it should be placed *outside* the end quotation marks.

Did she say, "I have to go to the store"?

I'm tired of being told that my writing is "adequate"!

Always place semicolons *outside* the end quotation mark.

O. Henry's most famous short story is "The Gift of the Magi"; like his others, it has a surprise ending.

The Russian delegate's vote was a loud "Nyet!"; as a result, the resolution was vetoed.

Use single quotation marks around quoted material within a direct quotation.

"We object to 'In God We Trust' on our currency," the lawyer stated.

"My favorite poem is 'Trees,' " said Royce.

FOR WORDS AND DEFINITIONS   Use quotation marks to call attention to words used in an unusual sense and in definitions.

I like the music of the Punks; my brother calls it "cacophony."

The origin of the word "bedlam" is interesting.

The Spanish expression "Adios" comes from another expression meaning "Go with God."

NOTE: *Many writers prefer to italicize (underline) words when used in this sense.*

FOR TITLES OF LITERARY AND ARTISTIC WORKS Use quotation marks to enclose titles of short poems, paintings, magazine articles, television programs, short stories, songs, and any selections from a longer work.

Poems:	''Crossing Brooklyn Ferry''
	''Chicago''
Paintings:	''The Last Supper''
	''Whistler's Mother''
Articles:	''How to Be a Better Husband''
	''Princess Diana: Is She Happy?''
Television Programs:	''Sixty Minutes''
	''NBC Evening News''
Short Stories:	''The Dead''
	''The Legend of Sleepy Hollow''
Songs:	''Stardust''
	''Caminos Verdes''

Italics

When words that would be italicized when printed are typed or handwritten, they should be underlined.

Underline (italicize) the titles of books, plays, magazines, newspapers, movies, long poems, and the names of ships, airplanes, and trains.

Books:	*Writing for College: A Practical Approach*
	The Grapes of Wrath
Plays:	*Romeo and Juliet*
	Our Town
Magazines:	*Newsweek*
	Surfer
Newspapers:	*Los Angeles Times*
	St. Louis Post-Dispatch
Movies:	*Revenge of the Nerds*
	Gone With the Wind
Long Poems:	*The Iliad*
	Paradise Lost
Ships:	*Old Ironsides*
	Queen Mary
Airplanes:	*Spirit of St. Louis*
	Enola Gay
Trains:	*Silver Bullet*
	Wabash Cannonball

Underline (italicize) foreign words and phrases that have not yet been adopted as English expressions. If you are not certain about the current status of a particular word or phrase, use a good modern dictionary.

caveat emptor

mea culpa

pro bono publico

Underline (italicize) when referring to letters, numbers, and words.

Carlos received two *B*'s and two *A*'s this semester.

Several American entrants were awarded *10*'s in the gymnastics competition.

The word *mischievous* is frequently mispronounced by speakers. (As noted above, some writers prefer to enclose words used like this in quotation marks.)

Underline (italicize) words that receive special emphasis.

He lives in Manhattan, *Kansas,* not Manhattan, *New York.*

Exercise 9:

Supply missing commas and quotation marks, and underline (italicize) where appropriate in the following sentences.

1. The expression to love, honor, and obey has been deleted from some marriage ceremonies.

2. Who was it that said, Don't shoot until you see the whites of their eyes?

3. The zeitgeist or feeling of the era during the 1920s was one of hedonism and self-indulgence.

4. My professor complained that several students confuse the words to, two, and too.

5. Although the movie Raiders of the Lost Ark was unbelievable, it had a few scenes that held my attention.

6. I enjoy reading George Wills' column in Newsweek magazine, and I always watch him on television when he appears on David Brinkley's Journal.

7. His father-in-law was a reporter for the Louisville Courier-Journal.

8. Professor McAndrews told us that the Broadway musical play Kiss Me Kate is based on Shakespeare's Taming of the Shrew.

9. The Greek letter rho looks like the Roman letter p.

10. My favorite poem said Aunt Agnes is Birches.

The Hyphen

The most common use of the hyphen is to break a word at the end of a line when there isn't enough room for the entire word. The hyphen has several other important uses, however.

The hyphen is used to set off certain prefixes.

1. After *ex-*, *self-*, and *all-* when they are used as prefixes.

   ex-player
   self-destructive
   all-purpose

2. After prefixes that precede a proper noun or adjective.

   anti-Semitic
   pro-French
   un-American
   pre-Christian
   trans-Atlantic

3. Between compound descriptions serving as a single adjective before a noun.

   wine-red sea
   soft-spoken cop
   slow-moving train

4. Between fractions and compound numbers from twenty-one through ninety-nine.

   three-fourths
   five-eighths
   fifty-four
   ninety-eight

The hyphen is used between syllables at the end of a line. Never divide a one-syllable word. When you are uncertain about the use of the hyphen in the syllabication of a word or in compound words, consult a collegiate-level dictionary.

The Apostrophe

The apostrophe is used for the possessive case (except for personal pronouns), to indicate an omitted letter or number, and to form the plural of numbers, specific words, and letters. Its use can be somewhat tricky at times, but by following the suggestions below, you will avoid the confusion that many writers have with the apostrophe.

1. Use the apostrophe to form the possessive case.
   a. To form the possessive case of a *singular* person, thing, or indefinite pronoun, add *'s*:

   the girl's identity

   the cat's meow

   Hank's razor

   everybody's obligation

   If a proper name already ends in *s* in its singular form and the adding of *'s* would make the pronunciation difficult, it is best to use the apostrophe only:

   Moses' teachings (Moses's *would be difficult to pronounce but is acceptable*)

   Tennessee Williams' plays (Williams's *would be acceptable but difficult to pronounce*)

   b. To form the possessive case of a plural noun ending in *s*, add an apostrophe only:

   the boys' bicycles

   the dogs' owners

   the soldiers' wives

   c. To form the possessive case of a plural noun *not* ending in *s*, add *'s*:

   women's rights

   children's television programs

   mice's tails

   d. To form the possessive of compound words, use the apostrophe according to the meaning of the construction:

   Simon and Garfunkel's records (the records that Simon and Garfunkel made together)

   Chaplin's and Woody Allen's movies (the movies of Chaplin and Allen, respectively)

Safeway's and Food Basket's competing sales campaigns (the separate sales campaigns of Safeway and Food Basket markets, respectively)

her mother and father's home (the home of her mother and father)

Steps for Forming Possessives of Nouns

1. Make the noun singular or plural, according to your meaning.
2. If the noun is singular, add *'s*. If adding the *'s* makes the pronunciation difficult, add an apostrophe only.
3. If the noun is plural and ends in *s*, just add an apostrophe. If the noun is plural and ends in some other letter, add *'s*.

---

2. Use an apostrophe to indicate an omitted letter or number.

   won't

   the '49ers

   'tis

3. Use an apostrophe to form the plurals of letters, specific words, and numbers.

   Watch your p's *and* q's.

   The yes's *outnumbered the* no's.

   Mike's lowest grade was in the 80's.

NOTE: *An apostrophe is not necessary for the plural of a year.*

The 1930s are remembered today for the Great Depression.

Some writers prefer to form the plural of a number by merely adding *-s*, omitting the apostrophe:

The temperature yesterday was in the 70s.

Do not use an apostrophe when writing out a number in the plural:

(incorrect)   *several seven's and eight's*
 (correct)   *several sevens and eights*

4. Do not use an apostrophe with the possessive forms of personal and relative pronouns:

(incorrect)   *it's* (to show possession), *her's, your's, our's, who's* (to show possession)

(correct)   *its, hers, yours, ours, whose*

Remember that *its* indicates ownership, and *it's* is a contraction for *it is* or *it has.* Similarly, *who's* means *who is* or *who has.*

5. Indefinite pronouns form the possessive case by adding *'s*:

one's, *anyone*'s, *someone*'s, *everyone*'s, *somebody*'s *(and so on)*

Numbers

1. If a number requires no more than two words, it should be spelled out.

nine months later

forty-one dollars

eighteen billion light years

If a number requires more than two words, use figures.

690 tons

4¹/₂ pounds

1072 pages

2. Write out a number beginning a sentence.

(awkward)   *14 patients at Broadway Hospital were treated for food poisoning yesterday.*

(revised)   *Fourteen patients at Broadway Hospital were treated for food poisoning yesterday.*

3. Use figures when they are followed by *a.m.* or *p.m.*; write out whole hours.

6:30 a.m.,   12 a.m.,   5:45 p.m.

twelve noon, eight o'clock

Exercise 10:

Insert any omitted hyphens or apostrophes in the following sentences, and make any necessary corrections in the use of numbers, quotation marks or underlining.

1. The president elect was briefed by the Central Intelligence Agency prior to his inauguration.

2. 30 classes were canceled because of a cut in funds by the administration.

3. Its been so hot this summer that my radiator burst one of its hoses.

4. Many Europeans call the letter z zed or zeta.

5. Gilbert and Sullivans operetta The Mikado was performed by a local opera company last week.

6. Approximately 50 nays and 25 nos were recorded.

7. Every evening after dinner I walk two and two thirds miles.

8. Any politician who professes anti feminist views risks losing a sizeable portion of the electorate.

9. To everyones surprise the stock market rallied strongly yesterday.

10. Clarissa said that she was thirty nine and holding.

10

Review Exercise

On the line preceding each number write the letter of the sentence that is correctly punctuated.

__B__ 1. a. "We will now sing America the Beautiful, announced the choir director, and we want everyone to join us."
  b. "We will now sing 'America the Beautiful,' " announced the choir
director, "and we want everyone to join us."

_____ 2. a. Small towns lack what many of us confront every day: traffic snarls,
foul air, bad manners, and crime.
  b. Small towns lack what many of us confront every day; traffic snarls,
foul air, bad manners, and crime.

__B__ 3. a. Van took two years of German, and three years of mathematics as part
of his pre-med program.
  b. Van took two years of German and three years of mathematics as part
of his pre-med program.

__A__ 4. a. Allen shook his head in disbelief and asked, "Are you sure about
that?"
  b. Allen shook his head in disbelief and asked, "Are you sure about
that"?

_____ 5. a. The governor promised to nominate qualified Mexican-Americans, to
vacancies on the judicial committee.
  b. The governor promised to nominate qualified Mexican-Americans to
vacancies on the judicial committee.

__B__ 6. a. The English physician William Harvey discovered the circulation of the
blood.
  b. The English physician, William Harvey, discovered the circulation of
the blood.

_____ 7. a. Oakland, California is across the bay from San Francisco.
  b. Oakland, California, is across the bay from San Francisco.

_____ 8. a. The states with the largest area are Texas and Alaska.
  b. The states, with the largest area are: Texas and Alaska.

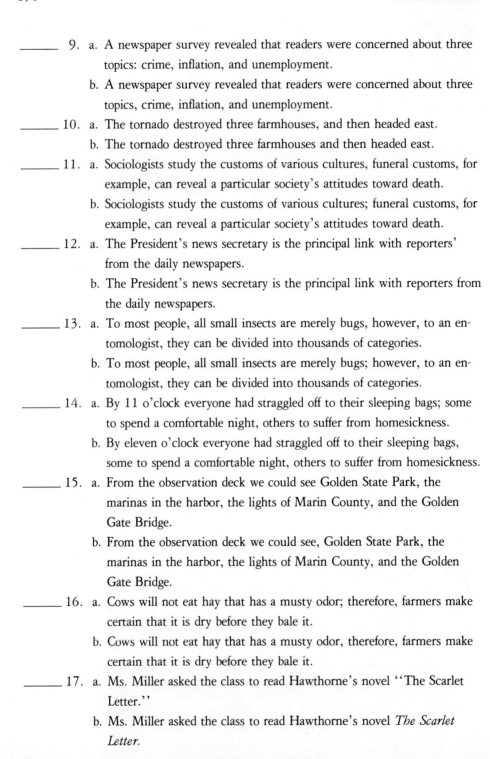

_____ 9. a. A newspaper survey revealed that readers were concerned about three topics: crime, inflation, and unemployment.

b. A newspaper survey revealed that readers were concerned about three topics, crime, inflation, and unemployment.

_____ 10. a. The tornado destroyed three farmhouses, and then headed east.

b. The tornado destroyed three farmhouses and then headed east.

_____ 11. a. Sociologists study the customs of various cultures, funeral customs, for example, can reveal a particular society's attitudes toward death.

b. Sociologists study the customs of various cultures; funeral customs, for example, can reveal a particular society's attitudes toward death.

_____ 12. a. The President's news secretary is the principal link with reporters' from the daily newspapers.

b. The President's news secretary is the principal link with reporters from the daily newspapers.

_____ 13. a. To most people, all small insects are merely bugs, however, to an entomologist, they can be divided into thousands of categories.

b. To most people, all small insects are merely bugs; however, to an entomologist, they can be divided into thousands of categories.

_____ 14. a. By 11 o'clock everyone had straggled off to their sleeping bags; some to spend a comfortable night, others to suffer from homesickness.

b. By eleven o'clock everyone had straggled off to their sleeping bags, some to spend a comfortable night, others to suffer from homesickness.

_____ 15. a. From the observation deck we could see Golden State Park, the marinas in the harbor, the lights of Marin County, and the Golden Gate Bridge.

b. From the observation deck we could see, Golden State Park, the marinas in the harbor, the lights of Marin County, and the Golden Gate Bridge.

_____ 16. a. Cows will not eat hay that has a musty odor; therefore, farmers make certain that it is dry before they bale it.

b. Cows will not eat hay that has a musty odor, therefore, farmers make certain that it is dry before they bale it.

_____ 17. a. Ms. Miller asked the class to read Hawthorne's novel ''The Scarlet Letter.''

b. Ms. Miller asked the class to read Hawthorne's novel *The Scarlet Letter.*

_____ 18. a. According to an authority on American slang, the most common slang terms deal with money, sex, and drinking.

b. According to an authority on American slang, the most common slang terms deal with: money, sex, and drinking.

_____ 19. a. The form should be completed, signed, and returned no later than September 1, 1986, to the address on the application.

b. The form should be completed, signed, and returned, no later than September 1, 1986 to the address on the application.

_____ 20. a. Some authorities believe that the best method of treating drug addiction is an immediate crash program, others, however, disagree.

b. Some authorities believe that the best method of treating drug addiction is an immediate crash program; others, however, disagree.

_____ 21. a. His wallet, which contained ninety dollars, was returned by the finder.

b. His wallet which contained ninety dollars was returned by the finder.

_____ 22. a. Besides beautiful scenery natural resources in the county include caves, subterranean lakes, and clear streams.

b. Besides beautiful scenery, natural resources in the county include caves, subterranean lakes, and clear streams.

_____ 23. a. Although the trip usually took only two days, we allowed ourselves a week.

b. Although the trip usually took only two day's we allowed ourselves a week.

_____ 24. a. The explorers followed the river to it's source in the mountains.

b. The explorers followed the river to its source in the mountains.

_____ 25. a. "A return to the gold standard," said the economist, "would produce a sound currency."

b. "A return to the gold standard," said the economist. "Would produce a sound currency."

SENTENCE COMBINING WITH INFINITIVES

An infinitive (page 25) is the "to" form of the verb: *to run, to hesitate, to bring, to think,* and so on. One of the most effective ways of combining sentences is to reduce or condense a simple sentence into an infinitive and combine it with another simple sentence.

1. *You should teach your children several things. They should not accept rides or money from anyone without your permission. They should tell a police officer if someone makes them feel scared. They should walk with friends to school and home.*

(combined)   *You should teach your children not* to accept *rides or money from anyone without your permission,* to tell *a police officer if someone makes them feel scared, and* to walk *with friends to school and home.*

2. *Norman has given up smoking. He wants to improve his health.*

(combined)   To improve *his health, Norman has given up smoking.*

3. *We wanted to get good seats for the game. We arrived at the stadium early.*

(combined)   To get *good seats for the game, we arrived at the stadium early.*

Combine the following sets of sentences by using infinitives. Underline the infinitives.

1. Greg had a fantasy. It was to live aboard a yacht berthed in the harbor.

2. Josie wanted to get married. She wanted to finish her degree. She wanted to have several children. She wanted to get a job and make a lot of money.

3. The tenor prepared for his role by hiring a voice coach. The coach helped him learn the part in the opera.

4. Milt calculated the volume of the tank by measuring its width, depth, and length. He calculated its weight in the same way.

5. Ray knew that he would look foolish if he wore a suit to the picnic. If he wanted to be comfortable, he should wear a pair of shorts.

Writing Original Sentences with Infinitives

Write ten original sentences, using infinitives. Underline the infinitives.

11

Capitalization

The capitalization of words helps the reader and serves as a guide to our meaning. The rules for capitalization are based, in general, on the following principle: the names of *specific* persons, places, and things (in other words, *proper* nouns) are capitalized; the names of *general* persons, places, and things *(common* nouns) are not capitalized.

1. Capitalize the first word in every sentence, including direct quotations that are complete sentences.

   It has snowed for six days and five nights.

   Have you washed the dishes?

   I can't believe it!

   Mr. Cassidy said, "My watermelon has too much salt on it."

2. Capitalize the first and last words in a title and all other words except *a, an, the,* and unimportant words with fewer than five letters.

   How to Be a Millionaire Without Really Trying

   A Farewell to Arms

   Everything You Always Wanted to Know About Sex
   But Were Afraid to Ask

3. Capitalize the titles of relatives and professions when they precede the person's name, or when they are used to address the person.

   Happy anniversary, Mother and Dad.

   My Uncle Patrick was a mail carrier for thirty years.

   My advisor is Professor Dreyfus.

   I have an appointment with Doctor Shelby tomorrow.

   Do *not* capitalize titles of relatives and professions when they are preceded by possessives (such as *my, your, his, our,* and *their)* and when they are used alone in place of the full name.

   My mother and father have been married forty years.

   My uncle is a retired mail carrier.

   My advisor is a professor of English.

   My doctor has an office downtown.

4. Capitalize official titles of honor and respect when they precede personal names.

   General George C. Marshall

   President Ronald Reagan

   Governor William Brennan

   Reverend Thomas J. Molloy

Ambassador Rodgers

Senator Jackson

Mayor Cisneros

Do *not* capitalize titles of honor and respect when they follow personal names.

a general in the United States Army

the governor of the state

an ambassador from Canada

the mayor of San Antonio

An exception to this rule is made for certain *national officials* (the President, Vice President, and Chief Justice) and *international figures* (the Pope, the Secretary General of the United Nations).

The President and the Vice President, with their wives, arrived in Rome last night and were greeted by the Pope and the Secretary General of the United Nations.

5. Capitalize the names of people, political, religious, and ethnic groups, languages, nationalities, and adjectives derived from them.

Japanese

Protestantism

Chicanos

Democrats

Communists

American

Victorian

Elizabethan

Canadians

Puritans

6. Capitalize the names of particular streets, buildings, bridges, rivers, cities, states, nations, specific geographical features, schools, and other institutions.

Broadway

Madison Avenue

Empire State Building

Brooklyn Bridge

Fox River

Osseo, Minnesota

Wheeling, West Virginia
Miami-Dade College
Sing Sing Prison
Uganda
Switzerland
Coney Island
Tellico Plains
Blue Ridge Mountains
University of North Carolina
Hofstra University
the United States House of Representatives
the United Nations

7. Capitalize directions only when they refer to specific regions or are part of a proper name.

out West
West Virginia
the Middle West
the West Coast
back East
the Near East
in the North
North Dakota

Do not capitalize these words when they merely indicate a direction or general location.

the western slope of the mountain
the south of Italy
facing north
northern Montana
on the east side of town

8. Capitalize the days of the week, months of the year, and names of holidays.

Friday
Good Friday
September
the Fourth of July

Father's Day
Passover
Veterans Day

9. Capitalize the names of particular historical events and eras.

the Civil War
World War I
the Great Depression
the Middle Ages
the Roaring Twenties

10. Capitalize the names of school subjects only if they are proper nouns or if they are followed by a course number.

anthropology
Anthropology 101
Portuguese
political science
Political Science 240a
American history
American History 152
psychology
Psychology 190

11. Capitalize all references to a supreme being.

God
the Almighty
the Holy Spirit
the Holy Ghost
the Lord
the Savior

Capitalize personal pronouns referring to a supreme being.

Ask God for His blessing.
Pray for His forgiveness.

Exercise 1:

Circle every letter or word that should be capitalized.

1. For my class in american literature professor bushman assigned a book by perry miller entitled *the new england mind: from colony to province.*

2. Shirley's mother is a physician at st. luke's hospital in santa monica, and her father is an accountant at bank of america.

3. The mayor of chicago made a bet with the mayor of detroit concerning the winner of the world's series to be played next october.

4. When I was a student at greenville community college, one of my classmates was the daughter of the governor of our state.

5. Many of the english people believe that the monarchy is an outmoded institution in the twentieth century.

6. Owners of cars parked on the northeast corner of lindell boulevard will be given citations except on holidays such as labor day and the fourth of july.

7. The communist party in italy is often in disagreement with the communist party in the soviet union over such matters as the proper relationship with the roman catholic church.

8. Every town seems to have a street called broadway or main. Growing up in st. louis, I often walked down broadway to the eads bridge which crossed the mississippi river.

9. The midwest is rich in history, beginning with the french fur traders and the jesuit priests who settled the mississippi valley.

10. I have never met the president of the united states, but I have watched him broadcast from the white house many times.

11

Review Exercise

Put an "X" next to the number of any word that should be capitalized.

1. Our art history class visited the (1) peabody Museum and heard a lecture by a (2) professor from (3) boston (4) university who discussed paintings of the (5) renaissance and the (6) seventeenth century.

   (1) _____ (2) _____ (3) _____ (4) _____ (5) _____ (6) _____

2. The (7) democratic party used to be a coalition of various ethnic and economic (8) groups; today, however, its support is dwindling among (9) unions and blue-collar workers.

   (7) _____ (8) _____ (9) _____

3. The (10) north and the (11) south, once bitter enemies, have virtually erased all traces of hostility created by the (12) civil (13) war and its bloody (14) battles that raged throughout the (15) southern part of the nation.

   (10) _____ (11) _____ (12) _____ (13) _____ (14) _____ (15) _____

4. At (16) veterans' cemeteries throughout the (17) country on (18) veterans (19) day, servicemen's (20) organizations pay tribute to those who died in battle.

   (16) _____ (17) _____ (18) _____ (19) _____ (20) _____

5. The instructor of my (21) geography class at my (22) community college received his master's degree from the (23) university (24) of (25) georgia.

   (21) _____ (22) _____ (23) _____ (24) _____ (25) _____

6. From what my (26) grandfather has told me, the music of the "big bands" was easy to dance to and was very melodic.

   (26) _____

7. New York City, which has a large (27) puerto rican population, is the largest city in the (28) eastern half of the country.

   (27) _____ (28) _____

8. Shelley's parents are   (29) baptists, but she is not a member of any particular   (30) church.

(29) _____ (30) _____

9. I could not remember the author of the novel   (31) *the*   (32) *return*
(33) *of*   (34) *the*   (35) *native.*

(31) _____ (32) _____ (33) _____ (34) _____ (35) _____

10. The   (36) island of   (37) corfu off the coast of   (38) greece is a favorite
vacation spot of the   (39) european   (40) socialites.

(36) _____ (37) _____ (38) _____ (39) _____ (40) _____

11. Don is a   (41) democrat and a   (42) liberal in his political views
concerning the role of the   (43) government in education.

(41) _____ (42) _____ (43) _____

12. Will you get a new job this   (44) summer, or will you work at the
(45) grocery story   (46) downtown on   (47) chestnut street?

(44) _____ (45) _____ (46) _____ (47)_____

13. Many people living in the   (48) northeast died during last   (49) winter's
freezing temperatures.

(48) _____ (49) _____

14. Please ask the   (50) doctor to sign this insurance form.

(50) _____

ADDITIONAL SENTENCE COMBINING PRACTICE WITH DEPENDENT CLAUSES

This section provides additional sentence combining practice with dependent clauses.

Below you will find several groups of sentences. In each case, combine them into a complex sentence by changing a sentence into a noun clause, an adverb clause, or an adjective clause.

Remember two important punctuation rules when using dependent clauses: an introductory adverb clause should be followed by a comma, and nonessential adjective clauses should be set off by commas.

1. Pedro de Alvarado invaded El Salvador in 1524. He was met by stiff Indian resistance.

2. The Suez Canal links Europe and Asia. Thus, it continues to be a world hot spot.

3. A debate is raging over the relative contribution of heredity and environment to intelligence. The debate has raised several questions. The questions and their answers have profound social implications.

4. Males are not born with an innate tendency to be hunters and warriors. They are not born to be sexually and politically dominant over females.

5. Our universe came into being from seven to fifteen billion years ago. That is the theory of most cosmologists. The beginning was an initial ''big bang'' explosion.

Writing Original Sentences with Dependent Clauses

Write ten original complex sentences, using a variety of dependent clauses. Underline each dependent clause. If you need to review complex sentences, reread pages 114–22.

12

Spelling

Some people seem to be born good spellers just as some people are apparently born with perfect musical pitch. Others—and perhaps they are the majority—continue to be plagued by mistakes in spelling all of their lives, to their own embarrassment and the irritation of others. To be sure, mistakes in spelling are not as serious as errors in grammar, word choice, organization, or punctuation, but they are usually more noticeable, and therefore more annoying. Like errors in punctuation, they distract the readers and make them wonder about the writer's credibility and the accuracy of his or her ideas. Whether right or wrong, most people in our society—particularly employers, instructors, and others in positions of authority—regard misspelled words as symbols of carelessness and irresponsibility.

Poor spellers are not necessarily lacking in intelligence or linguistic skill. The poets William Butler Yeats and John Keats were both notoriously bad spellers. But that is no excuse for careless or indifferent attempts to spell a word correctly. Granted, the English language is full of irregularities and inconsistencies; many of the letters in our alphabet have more than one sound, many words have letters that are silent, and others have sounds for which there seem to be no letters. From all of this, one might think that the English spelling system is all chaos and that it is impossible to determine and apply any rules with consistency. The fact is, however, that there *are* some rules and study techniques that will help to improve the spelling skills of even the least confident speller.

SOME SUGGESTIONS

If you are a weak speller, the first and probably most important suggestion for reducing the number of misspellings in your writing is to proofread your papers at least once, looking closely and carefully for words whose spelling you are uncertain of. Too often, students will guess at the spelling of a word or settle for an approximate version, hoping that the instructor will appreciate their creativity and imagination. But a series of misspelled words in an otherwise excellent paper is like spinach in your sweetheart's teeth: it does not enhance the subject. By looking over your papers carefully you will detect some misspelled words. You may even find it helpful to have a friend read over your work, since writers are often blind to their own mistakes.

Keeping a list of troublesome words is another way of pinpointing and reducing the number of misspelled words that can occur in writing. Such a list would have not only the correctly spelled form of the word, but also its meaning. By training your eye and exercising your curiosity, you will notice the individual quirks and characteristics of words, including their spelling. Of course, having a good college-level dictionary at hand when writing is important, and using it is even more helpful. If your instructor permits, bring your dictionary to class when writing your themes and compositions.

FOUR SPELLING RULES THAT USUALLY WORK

1. *ie* and *ei*

   When *ie* and *ei* have the long *e* sound (as in *meet),* use *i* before *e* except after *c.* The old jingle will help:

   Put i *before* e
   Except after c
   or when sounded like a
   As neighbor *and* weigh.

IE	EI (AFTER C)	EI (THE SOUND OF AY)
believe	ceiling	freight
cashier	conceit	neighbor
grief	perceive	sleigh
niece	receive	veil
shriek		vein
thief		weigh

   Some exceptions: *ancient, conscience, either, fiery, foreign, leisure, neither, seize, species, weird*

2. the silent final *e*

   If a word ends in a silent *e* (as in *hope),* drop the *e* before adding any ending that begins with a vowel. Keep the final *e* before endings that begin with a consonant.

BEFORE A VOWEL	BEFORE A CONSONANT
value + able = valuable	hope + ful = hopeful
hope + ed = hoped	sincere + ly = sincerely
give + ing = giving	nine + teen = nineteen
assure + ance = assurance	state + ment = statement
extreme + ity = extremity	love + ly = lovely
fate + at = fatal	

   Some exceptions: *dyeing, hoeing, duly (due + ly), truly (true + ly), noticeable, peaceable, courageous*

3. doubling the final consonant

   If a word of one syllable ends with a single consonant preceded by a single vowel (as in *hit),* double the final consonant before adding a suffix beginning with a vowel. If the word has more than one syllable, the emphasis should be on the final syllable.

SINGLE SYLLABLE	MULTISYLLABLE
hit + ing = hitting	admit + ed = admitted
slam + ed = slammed	permit + ing = permitting
stop + ed = stopped	repel + ing = repelling
fat + est = fattest	begin + er = beginner
fun + y = funny	prefer + ed = preferred

Some exceptions: *preference, conference, benefited, signaled (also spelled signalled)*

4. final *y*

When a word ends with *-y* preceded by a consonant, change the *y* to an *i* when adding a suffix, except those suffixes beginning with an *i:*

baby + es = babies

twenty + eth = twentieth

likely + hood = likelihood

marry + age = marriage *(but* marry + ing = marrying)

weary + ness = weariness

When a word ends with *-y* preceded by a vowel, do not change the *y:*

boy + s = boys

monkey + s = monkeys

attorney + s = attorneys

play + ed = played

Some exceptions: *paid, daily, said, laid*

FORMING THE PLURALS OF WORDS

Most words form their plurals by adding *s* to the singular:

announcements

bumblebees

cats

Words ending in *s, ch, sh,* or *x* add *es* to the singular:

glasses

churches

marshes

axes

The plural of hyphenated nouns is formed by adding *s* to the main noun:

mother-in-law = mothers-in-law

court-martial = courts-martial

Nouns ending with *ful* form their plural by adding *s* to the end of the word:

spoonful = spoonfuls   handful = handfuls

cupful = cupfuls

Some words ending in *f* change to *v* in the plural:

elf = elves

wife = wives   half = halves

leaf = leaves   life = lives

Some exceptions: *roofs, chiefs*

The plural of many nouns that end with *o* is formed by adding *s* if the *o* is preceded by another vowel:

radio = radios   ratio = ratios

studio = studios   zoo = zoos

The plural of many nouns that end with *o* is formed by adding *es* if the *o* is preceded by a consonant:

cargo = cargoes   motto = mottoes

echo = echoes   potato = potatoes

hero = heroes   zero = zeroes

The singular and the plural of some nouns are the same:

fish   series

deer   means

sheep

The plural of some nouns is formed by a change in spelling:

man = men   foot = feet

child = children   tooth = teeth

Plurals of nouns borrowed from other languages are usually formed according to the rules of those languages. You must memorize their plural forms or use a modern dictionary to check their current status. Here are some examples:

alumna = alumnae

alumnus = alumni

analysis = analyses

basis = bases

crisis = crises

criterion = criteria

datum = data

dictum = dicta

memorandum = memoranda

parenthesis = parentheses

TWENTY-FIVE SETS OF HOMONYMS: WORDS OFTEN CONFUSED

Many words in the English language are often confused because they sound the same (or almost the same) as other words. Such words are *homonyms,* and the list that follows contains some of those that are most frequently misused by writers.

Look the list over carefully, noting the differences in meaning. For additional words that are often confused, see ''A Glossary of Usage'' on page 222.

All ready and **already**	*All ready* is an adjective meaning ''entirely ready.'' We are packed and *all ready* to go. *Already* is an adverb meaning ''previously.'' Jack pretended to be surprised, but he had *already* heard about the party.
All together and **altogether**	*All together* means ''in a group.'' The families of the bride and groom were *all together* in the reception area. *Altogether* means ''completely'' or ''entirely.'' We were *altogether* exhausted after the trek through the desert.
Bare and **bear**	*Bare* is an adjective meaning ''naked'' or ''undisguised.'' The baby wiggled out of its diaper and was completely *bare. Bear* as a verb means ''to carry or support.'' As a noun it refers to ''a large omnivorous animal.'' The bridge was too weak to *bear* the weight of the trucks. While we were in Yosemite, we saw several large *bears* foraging for food in a nearby campground.
Buy and **by**	*Buy* is a verb meaning ''to purchase.'' When you *buy* a home, you are probably making the largest purchase of your life. *By* is a preposition meaning ''close to or next to.'' An old Pontiac was parked *by* the shed.

Capital and **capitol**	*Capital* is the leading city of a state, or wealth, or chief in importance.
	The *capital* of Spain is Madrid.
	Ted lives on the interest from his accumulated *capital.*
	The low interest rate was of *capital* importance in holding down inflation.
	Capitol is the building in which lawmakers sit.
	The flag of surrender flew over the *capitol.*
Coarse and **course**	*Coarse* is an adjective meaning ''rough'' or ''inferior.''
	The sandpaper was too *coarse* to use on the table.
	Course is a noun meaning ''direction'' or ''academic studies.''
	By using a compass, we were able to follow the right *course.*
	The *course* in statistics was helpful in my job later.
Complement and **compliment**	*To complement* is ''to balance or complete.''
	Brian's new tie *complemented* his suit.
	To compliment is ''to flatter.'' As a noun it means ''an expression of praise.''
	When anyone *complimented* Bernice, she blushed, because she was unaccustomed to *compliments.*
Consul, council, and **counsel**	A *consul* is a government official stationed in another country.
	The American *consul* in Paris helped the stranded New Yorkers locate their family.
	A *council* is a body of people acting in an official capacity.
	The city *council* passed a zoning regulation.
	Counsel as a noun means ''an advisor'' or ''advice''; as a verb it means ''to advise.''
	The defendant's *counsel* objected to the question.
	The *counsel* that he gave her was based on his many years of experience.
	Marvin *counseled* me on my decision.
Forth and **fourth**	*Forth* is an adverb meaning ''forward in time or place.''
	When the doors opened, the mob rushed *forth.*
	Fourth is an adjective form of ''four,'' the number.
	On my *fourth* attempt, the car finally started.
Hear and **here**	*Hear* is a verb meaning ''to listen to.''
	From our room we could *hear* the roar of the crowd.

© 1986 Scott, Foresman and Company

	Here is an adverb meaning "in this place."
	A new restaurant will be opened *here* next week.
Hole and **whole**	*Hole* is a noun meaning "a cavity."
	The acid etched a *hole* in the coin.
	Whole as an adjective means "complete or healthy"; as a noun it means "all of the components or parts of a thing."
	I ate the *whole* thing.
	Her performance as a *whole* was rated superior.
It's and **its**	*It's* is a contraction for "it is" or "it has."
	It's quite an accomplishment, but I received a "C" in math.
	It's been a cool summer.
	Its is the possessive form of *It.*
	Every tool was in *its* proper place.
Knew and **new**	**Knew** is the past tense of *know.*
	Randy thought he *knew* the combination, but he had forgotten it.
	New means "recent."
	New evidence was discovered linking the two thieves.
No and **know**	*No* as an adverb means "not so"; as an adjective, it means "not any, not one."
	No, I did not receive my mail yet.
	We had *no* opportunity to tell Greg goodbye.
Peace and **piece**	*Peace* is a noun meaning "tranquility" or "the absence of war."
	The Prime Minister promised *peace* in our time.
	Piece as a noun means "a part or portion of something."
	Virginia preferred to get paid by the hour rather than by the *piece.*
Principal and **principle**	*Principal* as an adjective means "main," "chief"; as a noun it means "a sum of money" or "the head of a school."
	The *principal* reason she stayed was loyalty to her family.
	Scott repaid the *principal* of the loan and the interest within a month.
	The *principal* of my high school encouraged me to go to college.
	Principle is a noun meaning "a truth, rule, or code of conduct."
	I could never learn the *principles* of the slide rule.
	Gambling is based on the *principle* of greed.

Right and write	*Right* as a noun means ''a just claim or title'' or ''the right-hand side.''
	The *right* to worship freely is every American's legacy.
	In Ireland we could not drive on the *right*.
	Write means ''to draw or communicate.''
	Ben was able to *write* at the age of four.
Role and roll	*Role* is a noun meaning ''a part or function.''
	The navy's *role* in the revolution was unclear.
	Roll as a verb means ''to move forward, as on wheels''; as a noun, it means ''bread'' or ''a list of names.''
	The tanks *rolled* down the main street of the town.
	Professor Lewis often forgets to take *roll*.
Scene and seen	*Scene* is a noun meaning ''a view or setting.''
	The *scene* from my hotel room was unforgettable.
	Seen is the past participle of *see*.
	Have you ever *seen* a falling star?
Stationary and stationery	*Stationary* is an adjective meaning ''permanent'' or ''not moving.''
	The wheels of the car were locked in a *stationary* position.
	Stationery is a noun meaning ''writing paper and envelopes.''
	Lois gave me a box of monogrammed *stationery*.
There, their, and they're	*There* is an adverb meaning ''in that place.''
	Place the packages *there* on the table.
	Their is the possessive form of *they*.
	They were shocked to find *their* house on fire.
	They're is a contraction of *they are*.
	They're usually late for every party.
To, too, and two	*To* is a preposition; *too* is an adverb; *two* is an adjective.
	He ran *to* the door.
	I'm *too* excited to eat.
	It snowed heavily *two* days ago.
Weather and whether	*Weather* is a noun referring to climatic conditions.
	If we have warm *weather* tomorrow, let's eat outdoors.
	Whether is a conjunction that introduces alternatives.
	It may rain tomorrow *whether* we like it or not.

Whose and **who's**	*Whose* is the possessive form of *who*.
	Whose car is in my parking space?
	Who's is a contraction for *who is* or *who has*.
	Who's at the door?
	Who's been eating my porridge?
Your and **you're**	*Your* is the possessive form of *you*.
	Are these *your* gloves?
	You're is a contraction for *you are*.
	You're in trouble.

SPELLING LIST

Here is a list of words commonly misspelled in college students' writing. Study these words carefully and memorize the spelling of any you are not sure of.

ably	almost	benefited
absence	allowed	boundary
abundance	altar	breath
academic	alter	breathe
accept	altogether	bureau
accidentally	amateur	business
accommodate	analysis	cafeteria
accommodation	analyze	calendar
accompanied	anonymous	campaign
accuracy	anxiety	candidate
achieve	apparatus	capital
achievement	apparent	capitol
acknowledge	appearance	career
acquaintance	arguing	carrying
acquired	argument	ceiling
across	athletic	cemetery
address	audience	certain
adequate	awkward	chief
admittance	bachelor	chosen
advice	basically	column
affect	beautiful	coming
aggravate	becoming	committee
aging	beginning	competent
all right	believed	competition

condemn	excellent	hurriedly
conscientious	exercise	hygiene
conscious	exhaust	hypocrisy
continuous	existence	imitation
criticism	explanation	immense
criticize	familiar	incidentally
deceive	fantasy	incredible
decision	fascinate	indefinite
definitely	February	independence
definition	fictitious	innocence
dependent	fiery	inquiry
desirable	finally	insistence
desperate	financially	intelligence
devastating	forehead	intercede
development	foreign	interfere
difference	foremost	irrelevant
dining	forth	irresistible
disappear	forty	its
disappoint	fourth	it's
disastrous	fulfill	jealous
disease	gases	judgment
dissatisfied	gauge	*(also* judgement)
divide	glamorous	knowledge
doesn't	government	laboratory
echoes	grammar	legitimate
effect	grievance	leisure
efficient	grievous	lessen
eighth	guarantee	lesson
eligible	guard	library
eliminate	guidance	license
embarrass	happily	lightning
emphasize	happiness	likely
enthusiastic	harass	literature
environment	height	loneliness
equipped	heroes	loose
exaggerate	humorous	lose

losing	presence	specimen
maintenance	prevalent	studying
maneuver	privilege	succeed
marriage	probably	surprise
mathematics	procedure	susceptible
medicine	prominent	technique
mileage	pronunciation	temperament
mischievous	psychology	tendency
moral	pursue	theory
morale	quantity	therefore
mountain	questionnaire	thorough
muscle	realize	throughout
musician	recede	truly
mysterious	recommend	Tuesday
naturally	rehearsal	twelfth
necessary	religious	unanimous
ninety	reminiscence	unnecessary
noticeable	repetition	unusual
obstacle	restaurant	unusually
occasion	rhythm	usage
occasionally	ridiculous	using
occurred	sacrifice	vacuum
occurrence	safety	valuable
omission	salary	village
omitted	Saturday	villain
opposed	scarcely	visible
optimistic	schedule	warring
parallel	science	weather
pastime	secretary	Wednesday
permissible	seize	whether
personnel	separate	whisper
physician	sergeant	whole
pneumonia	severely	wholly
possess	similar	who's
preceding	skeptical	whose
prejudice	sophomore	women

writing
written
yield
your
you're

12

NAME   DATE

Review Exercise

A. On the line preceding each sentence, write the letter corresponding to the correct word.

_____ 1. The shoreline was (a. *already,* b. *all ready)* covered with oil when the leak in the well on the ocean floor was finally capped.

_____ 2. It was (a. *all together,* b. *altogether)* too early to predict the winner.

_____ 3. When Glen was a child, he wrote only in (a. *capital,* b. *capitol)* letters.

_____ 4. (a. *Coarses,* b. *Courses)* in computers are popping up everywhere.

_____ 5. Although I meant it as a (a. *complement,* b. *compliment)*, Harry was offended by my comment about his tie.

_____ 6. Mr. Doria can always be counted on to give me wise (a. *consul,* b. *counsel)*.

_____ 7. I realize (a. *it's,* b. *its)* a familiar excuse, but my bulldog ate my term paper.

_____ 8. One of the (a. *principal,* b. *principle)* reasons I can't save money is that I can't resist a bargain.

_____ 9. My history instructor accepts only typewritten work and refuses any papers that we (a. *right,* b. *write)* in ink.

_____ 10. Many Americans still debate the (a. *role,* b. *roll)* of our country in Vietnam.

_____ 11. Several travelers reported that (a. *their,* b. *they're)* passports were stolen.

_____ 12. Claiming that it was (a. *to,* b. *too)* heavy, the postal clerk refused to accept my package for delivery to San Francisco.

_____ 13. The (a. *weather,* b. *whether)* in Miami is affected by tropical currents.

_____ 14. A man (a. *whose,* b. *who's)* name I forgot left his telephone number for you.

_____ 15. A mutual friend told me that (a. *your,* b. *you're)* a good chess player.

B. On the line preceding each number, write the letter of the correctly spelled word.

	a.	b.	c.
_____ 16.	accidentally	acidentally	accidentaly
_____ 17.	accommodate	acommodate	accomodate
_____ 18.	acompanied	accompanied	accommpanied
_____ 19.	acheivment	achievment	achievement
_____ 20.	aquaintance	acquaintance	acquaintence
_____ 21.	appearence	appearance	apparance
_____ 22.	benefitted	benifited	benefited
_____ 23.	committee	comittee	commitee
_____ 24.	conscientious	concientious	consientious
_____ 25.	definitely	definitly	definetely
_____ 26.	desparate	desperate	desperete
_____ 27.	disappear	dissappear	disapear
_____ 28.	embarass	embarrass	emmbarrass
_____ 29.	exxagerate	exagerate	exaggerate
_____ 30.	goverment	governmant	government
_____ 31.	independence	independance	indepandance
_____ 32.	irrisistible	irresistible	iresistible
_____ 33.	leisure	liesure	leesure
_____ 34.	loneliness	lonliness	loniliness
_____ 35.	mathmatics	mathamatics	mathematics
_____ 36.	mischievious	mischevious	mischievous

_____ 37. necesary   necessary   neccessary

_____ 38. occassionally   occasionaly   occasionally

_____ 39. occurrence   ocurrence   occurrance

_____ 40. possess   posess   posses

_____ 41. privelege   privilege   privelige

_____ 42. questionnaire   questionaire   questionairre

_____ 43. reccomend   reccommend   recommend

_____ 44. relegious   religious   riligious

_____ 45. seperate   seperete   separate

_____ 46. therefor   therefore   therforе

_____ 47. truley   truly   truely

_____ 48. unnecessary   unecessary   unneccesary

_____ 49. useage   usaege   usage

_____ 50. wholely   wholly   wholy

SENTENCE COMBINING: A REVIEW

This section will give you an opportunity to review the many sentence combining techniques you have practiced in previous chapters.

Rewrite the following paragraphs so that their sentences are smoother and the relationship between their ideas is clearer. Use the sentence combining techniques that seem most appropriate.

1. Henry Wadsworth Longfellow wrote a poem. It is called "Paul Revere's Ride." It is filled with historical inaccuracies. The date was April 18, 1775. Two young men were sent out on horseback. They were to alert the American rebels between Boston and Lexington. One was Paul Revere. The other was an unknown shoemaker. His name was William Dawes. The commander of the Colonial forces was Joseph Warren. He sent Dawes along the land route to spread the word. Warren dispatched Revere along the water route. Revere got sidetracked. He was finally captured by the British near the end of his ride. Dawes rode first. He rode the longest distance. He carried out his assignment. Today no one remembers him. The only one that is remembered is Paul Revere.

2. Little League baseball originated in Williamsport, Pennsylvania. The year was 1939. There were three teams. Today the program is worldwide. It provides girls and boys from eight to eighteen with supervised sports activity. It involves thirty countries and more than nine thousand leagues. This is in addition to thousands of adult volunteers. The first official Little League World Series was held in 1947. It was held in Williamsport. The popularity of the Little League World Series spread rapidly. This was due to the success of that first tournament.

3. The soybean is the most important bean in the world. It was cultivated in China before 3500 B.C. It was unknown in Europe and the United States until 1900. There are about thirty varieties. The one that most Americans are familiar with is yellow. The soybean is the only true meat substitute in the legume family. It provides complete protein as well as essential amino acids, calcium, and B vitamins. Soybeans are able to provide a cheap and nutritional diet. This is important for the underdeveloped countries. Soybeans are able to serve as meat substitutes for wealthier countries. Soybeans are also made into flour. They are broken up into grits. They are also broken up into a curd called "tofu." Tofu is used extensively in Japanese and Chinese cooking. The versatility of this bean is unlimited. Our natural resources are becoming scarcer. We will discover the true worth of the soybean.

A Glossary of Usage

This glossary is an alphabetical guide to words that frequently cause problems
for writers. Some entries are labeled ''colloquial,'' and some ''nonstandard.''
A colloquialism is a word or phrase more appropriate to informal speech than
to writing. Although colloquialisms are not grammatically incorrect, they
should be avoided in formal writing, and even in informal writing they should
be used sparingly. A nonstandard word or phrase is avoided at all times by
careful speakers and writers. It is the kind of error sometimes labeled ''incorrect'' or ''illiterate.''

   If you want to know more about the words in this glossary, consult
Webster's Third *New International Dictionary* or a modern college-level dictionary. Other troublesome words that often cause problems for writers can be
found on pages 209–13 (''Twenty-five Sets of Homonyms: Words Often Confused'') in Chapter 12.

accept, except   *Accept* is a verb meaning ''to receive,'' and *except* is a preposition
   meaning ''but,'' or a verb meaning ''to exclude.'' ''I will *accept* your invitation.'' ''Everyone *except* Henry went.'' ''We voted to *except* the new
   members from the requirements.''

advice, advise   *Advice* is an opinion you offer; *advise* means to recommend. ''Her *advice* was always helpful.'' ''The counselor will *advise* you concerning the proper course to take.''

affect, effect   *To affect* is to change or modify; *to effect* is to bring about something;
   an *effect* is a result. ''The drought will *affect* the crop production.'' ''I hope
   the treatment will *effect* a change in his condition.'' ''The *effect* should be
   noticeable.''

aggravate, annoy   These two are often confused. *To aggravate* is to make a condition
   worse: ''The treatment only *aggravated* his condition.'' *To annoy* is to irritate: ''The ticking clock *annoyed* Dean as he read.''

agree to, agree with   You agree *to* a thing or plan: ''Mexico and the United States
   agree to the border treaty.'' You agree *with* a person: ''Laura and Herb
   agreed with each other over the price of the typewriter.''

ain't   Although *ain't* is in the dictionary, it is a nonstandard word never used by
   educated or careful speakers and writers except to achieve a deliberate
   humorous effect. The word should be avoided.

allusion, illusion   An *allusion* is an indirect reference to something: ''He made an
   allusion to his parents' wealth.'' An *illusion* is a false image or impression:
   ''It is an *illusion* to think that I will be a millionaire soon.''

among, between   Use *between* for two objects and *among* for more than two: ''The
   hummingbird darted *among* the flowers.'' ''I sat *between* my mother and
   father.''

amount, number   *Amount* refers to quantity or to things in the aggregate; *number* refers to countable objects: "A large *amount* of work remains to be done." "A *number* of jobs were still unfilled."

anyone, any one   *Anyone* means "any person at all": "I will talk to *anyone* who answers the telephone." *Any one* means any single person: "*Any one* of those players can teach you the game in a few minutes."

anyways, anywheres   These are nonstandard forms for *anyway* and *anywhere* and they should be avoided.

bad, badly   *Bad* is an adjective; *badly* is an adverb. "Her pride was hurt *badly* [not *bad*]." "She feels *bad* [not *badly*]"

being as, being that   These are nonstandard terms and should be avoided. Use *since* or *because.*

beside, besides   *Beside* is a preposition meaning "by the side of": "The doctor sat *beside* the bed talking to his patient." *Besides* may be a preposition or adverb meaning "in addition to" or "also": "*Besides* my homework, I have some letters to write."

between, among   See *among, between.*

breath, breathe   *Breathe* is the verb: "The air we *breathe* is contaminated with pollutants." *Breath* is the noun: "He tried to conceal the smell of alcohol on his *breath.*"

burst, bursted, bust, busted   *Burst* remains the same in the past, present, and past participle forms; *bursted, bust,* and *busted* are incorrect or nonstandard forms.

can, may   *Can* refers to ability; *may* refers to permission. "After taking only a few lessons, Tom *can* play the trumpet beautifully. Because of the neighbors, however, he *may* play only in the afternoon."

can't hardly, barely, scarcely   These are double negatives and are to be avoided. Use *can hardly, can barely,* and *can scarcely.*

can't help but   Avoid this expression. Use "can't help doing something" but not "can't help but do something."

conscience, conscious   A conscience is a sense of right or wrong: "His *conscience* wouldn't allow him to cheat on the exam." To be conscious is to be aware: "I was not *conscious* of the noise in the background."

continual, continuous   *Continual* means "repeated frequently," as in "We heard a series of *continual* beeps in the background." *Continuous* means "without interruption": "I was lulled to sleep by the *continuous* hum of the motor in the deck below."

could of   A nonstandard form. Use could *have:* "I could *have* gone with him if I wanted."

different from, than   One thing is different *from* another, not different *than.*

disinterested, uninterested   To be *disinterested* is to be impartial: "The judge was a *disinterested* listener in the case." To be *uninterested* is to lack interest: "It was obvious that Jack was *uninterested* in the lecture because he dozed off several times.''

double negative   Unacceptable in formal writing and in most informal situations except for humorous effect. Double negatives range from such obvious errors as ''I don't have no paper'' to more subtle violations (''I can't scarcely'' and ''It isn't hardly''). Avoid them.

due to, because of   In formal writing, use *due to* after any form of the verb *be (am, are, is, was,* and so on): ''My headache is *due to* not eating breakfast or lunch.'' Use *because of* in other situations: *''Because of* my diet, I often have a headache.''

enormity, enormousness   *Enormity* means ''atrociousness''; *enormousness* means ''of great size.'' ''The *enormity* of the crime shocked the hardened crime reporters.'' ''Because of the *enormousness* of the ship, it could not be docked in the local harbor.''

enthused   Nonstandard. Use ''enthusiastic'' (''He was *enthusiastic* about our plans for next summer,'' *not* ''He was *enthused* about our plans for next summer.'')

farther, further   Use *farther* for physical distance (''They live *farther* from town than we do'') and *further* for degree or quantity (''Their proposal was a *further* attempt to reach an agreement'').

fewer, less   Use *fewer* for items that can be counted, and *less* for quantity: *''Fewer* jobs are available for young people this summer.'' ''He paid *less* for that car than I paid for mine.''

good, well   *Good* is an adjective, never an adverb. ''She performs *well* [not *good]* in that role.'' *Well* is an adverb and an adjective; in the latter case it means ''in a state of good health'': ''I am *well* now, although last week I didn't feel very *good.''* See Chapter 9.

hanged, hung   Criminals are *hanged;* pictures are *hung.*

hisself   A nonstandard term. Use *himself.*

if, whether   Use *if* to introduce a clause implying a condition: *''If* you go to summer school, you can graduate early.'' Use *whether* to introduce a clause implying a choice: ''I'm not sure *whether* I will go to summer school.''

imply, infer   ''To imply'' is to hint strongly; ''to infer'' is to derive the meaning from someone's statement by deduction. You *infer* the meaning of a passage when you read or hear it; the writer or speaker *implies* it.

irregardless   Nonstandard. Use *regardless.*

is when, is where   Avoid these expressions to introduce definitions, as in ''A sonnet is when you have fourteen lines of iambic pentameter in a prescribed rhyme scheme.'' Better, ''A sonnet is a poem with fourteen lines of iambic pentameter in a prescribed rhyme scheme.''

kind of, sort of   These are colloquial expressions acceptable in informal speech, but not in writing. Use ''somewhat'' or ''rather'' instead.

leave, let   *Leave* means "to go away," and *let* means "to allow." Do not use *leave* for *let*. "Please *let* [not *leave*] me go."

liable, likely, apt   *Liable* means "legally responsible" or "susceptible to"; *likely* means "probably," and *apt* refers to a talent or a tendency. "He is *liable* for the damage he caused." "Those clouds indicate it's *likely* to rain this afternoon." "She is an *apt* tennis player."

like   *Like* is a noun, verb, adjective, and preposition; do not use it as a conjunction: "He acted as if (not *like*) he wanted to go with us."

loose, lose   "To loosen" means to untie or unfasten; "to lose" is to misplace. *Loose* as an adjective means "unfastened" or "unattached." "He *loosened* his necktie." "Did he *lose* his necktie?" "His necktie is *loose.*"

maybe, may be   *Maybe* means "perhaps"; *may be* is a verb phrase. "*Maybe* we'll win tomorrow." "It *may be* that we'll win tomorrow."

must of   Nonstandard. Write (and say) "must have," and in similar constructions use "could have" (not "could of") or "would have" (not "would of").

myself   *Myself* is correct when used as an intensive or reflexive pronoun ("I helped *myself* to the pie," and "I hurt *myself*"), but it is used incorrectly as a substitute for *I* and *me* as in the following: "My brother and *myself* were in the army together in Germany." "They spoke to George and *myself* about the matter."

precede, proceed   To *precede* is "to go before or in front of"; to *proceed* is "to continue moving ahead." "Poverty and hunger often *precede* a revolution." "They *proceeded* down the aisle as if nothing had happened."

quiet, quite, quit   Read the following sentences to note the differences: "I wanted to get away from the noise and find a *quiet* spot." "They are *quite* upset that their son married without their permission." "When college starts next fall, he will *quit* his summer job."

raise, rise   *Raise* is a verb meaning "to lift or help to rise in a standing position." Its principal parts are *raised, raised,* and *raising. Rise* means "to assume an upright position" or "to wake up"; its principle parts are *rose, risen,* and *rising.*

set, sit   *To sit* means "to occupy a seat"; the principal parts are *sat, sat,* and *sitting. Set* means "to place something somewhere," and its principal parts are *set, set,* and *setting.* See Chapter 6.

shall, will   Most authorities, writers, and speakers use these interchangeably. Follow the advice of your instructor.

somewheres   Nonstandard. Use "somewhere"; similarly, avoid *nowheres.*

theirselves   A nonstandard term. Use *themselves.*

© 1986 Scott, Foresman and Company

A Glossary of Grammatical Terms

This glossary is an alphabetical guide to the grammatical terms used in this book, as well as to other helpful words. Some entries contain references to other terms or to sections of the text in which they are discussed in detail. For further references and explanation you should consult the index.

abstract noun   A noun that refers to an idea or quality that cannot be identified by one of the senses. *Shame; delight; tolerance*   See *concrete noun.*

action verb   See *verb.*

adjective   A word that modifies (limits or describes) a noun or pronoun. The concert was *long,* but it was *exciting.* (The adjective *long* modifies the noun *concert,* and the adjective *exciting* modifies the pronoun *it.)* See Chapter 1.

adjective clause   A dependent clause that modifies a noun or pronoun. The delegates *who voted for the amendment* changed their minds. (The adjective clause modifies the noun *delegates.)* See Chapter 7.

adverb   A word that modifies (limits or describes) an adjective, a verb, or another adverb. She cried *softly. (Softly* modifies the verb *cried.)* They are *extremely* wealthy. *(Extremely* modifies the adjective *wealthy.)* He left the room *very* hurriedly. *(Very* modifies the adverb *hurriedly.)* See Chapter 1.

adverb clause   A dependent clause that modifies an adjective, verb, or another adverb. I think of her *when I hear that song.* (The adverb clause modifies the verb *think.)* He became angry *because he had forgotten his keys.* (The adverb clause modifies the adjective *angry.)* The band played so loudly *that I got a headache.* (The adverb clause modifies the adverb *so.)* See Chapter 7.

agreement   The correspondence of one word with another, particularly subjects with verbs and pronouns with antecedents. If the subject of a sentence is singular, the verb is singular (''My *tire is* flat''); if the subject is singular, pronouns referring to it should also be singular (''The *carpenter* forgot *his* hammer''). Plural subjects require plural verbs and plural pronouns are used to refer to plural antecedents. See Chapters 3 and 5.

antecedent   A word or group of words a pronoun refers to. Jimmy, *who* used to play in a rock group, decided *he* would go back to college to complete *his* degree. *(Who, he,* and *his* all refer to the antecedent *Jimmy.)* See Chapter 5.

appositive   A word or phrase following a noun or pronoun which renames or explains it. London, *the capital,* was bombed heavily. The author *Mark Twain* lived in Connecticut. In the first example, *the capital* is a nonessential appositive because it is not needed to identify the word it follows. In the second example, *Mark Twain* is an essential appositive because it is needed to identify the general term *author.* Only nonessential appositives are set off by commas. See Chapter 10.

article   *A, an,* and *the* are articles. *A* and *an* are indefinite articles; *the* is a definite article. Articles are usually regarded as adjectives because they precede nouns.

auxiliary verb   A helping verb used to form verb phrases. The most common auxiliary verbs are forms of *be* ("am," "are," "is," "have been," and so on) and *have* ("had," "has," and so on); others include the various forms of *do, can, shall, will, would, could, should, may, might,* and *must.* See Chapters 1 and 2.

case   The form of a pronoun or noun to show its use in a sentence. Pronouns have three cases: the *nominative* or subject case *(I, he, she, they,* and so on), the *objective* case *(me, him, her, them,* and so on), and the *possessive (my, his, her, their,* and so on). Nouns change their spelling only in the possessive case *(Larry's, man's,* and so on). See Chapter 4.

clause   A group of words containing a subject and a verb. A clause may be either independent or dependent. Independent clauses may stand alone as simple sentences. The dependent clause must be joined to an independent clause. "The restaurant was closed by the health department *(independent clause)* because the chef had hepatitis *(dependent clause)."* See Chapters 2 and 7.

collective noun   A noun that names a group of persons or things, such as *army, committee, flock.* Collective nouns usually take singular verbs ("The troop *was* ready to leave") except when the individual members are thought of ("The class *were* arguing among themselves"). See Chapter 3.

colloquialism   An informal word or expression more appropriate to speech than to writing.

comma-splice   The misuse of a comma between two independent clauses in a compound sentence: "Herb's brother studied architecture in college, he designed the new office building downtown." Comma-splices can be corrected by substituting a semicolon for the comma or by inserting a coordinating conjunction after the comma. See Chapter 8.

command   See *imperative sentence.*

common noun   A noun that names a general category or class of persons, places, or things: *city, tool, song.* Common nouns are not capitalized except when they begin a sentence. See *proper noun* and Chapter 1.

comparative degree   The *more, less,* or *-er* form of those adjectives than can be compared.

comparison   The change in the spelling of adjectives and adverbs to show degree. The degrees of comparison in English are *positive (slowly, loud), comparative (more slowly, louder),* and *superlative (most slowly, loudest).* Some modifiers cannot be compared: *round, dead, unique, full,* and so on.

complement   A word or expression that completes the sense of a verb. See *direct object, indirect object, predicate adjective, predicate noun,* and *predicate pronoun.*

complex sentence   A sentence containing one independent clause and at least one dependent clause: "The grain embargo *which was announced last year* was criticized by the farmers." The dependent clause is italicized. See Chapter 7.

compound   Two or more words or word groups linked to form a single unit. For instance, two nouns can form a compound subject: *"Merchants and business-people* were united in their opposition to the new tax,'' and two verbs can function as a compound predicate: "She *danced and sang* in the leading role.''

compound-complex sentence   A sentence containing at least two independent clauses and one or more dependent clauses: "Although the demand for oil has declined, the price of gasoline continues to climb, and the OPEC nations threaten a new price hike.'' See Chapter 7.

compound sentence   A sentence with two or more independent clauses but no dependent clauses: "She wanted to read the book, but someone had previously borrowed it.'' See Chapter 7.

concrete noun   A noun naming something that can be perceived by one of the senses: butter, elevator, scream, buzz. See *abstract noun.*

conjunction   A word that connects words, phrases, and clauses. See *coordinate conjunction, subordinate conjunction,* and Chapter 1.

conjunctive adverb   An adverb that connects independent clauses after a semicolon: "I had looked forward to seeing the movie; *however,* after reading the reviews I changed my mind.'' See Chapter 8.

contraction   A word formed from the union of two words, with an apostrophe replacing the missing letters: *hasn't* (has not); *I'm* (I am).

coordinate adjectives   Two or more adjectives of equal importance that modify the same noun: "The *tall, scowling* doorman finally let us in.''

coordinate conjunction   A word that connects two or more words, phrases, or clauses of equal rank. The most common coordinate conjunctions are *and, but, for, or, nor, so.* See Chapter 1.

correlative conjunctions   Pairs of conjunctions used to join parts of a sentence of equal rank. The most common correlative conjunctions are *either . . . or; neither . . . nor; not only . . . but also; both . . . and.* See Chapters 1 and 9.

dangling modifier   A modifier that has no word in the sentence for it to modify. It is left "dangling" and consequently ends up modifying an unintended word, as in the following: "Raising his bow triumphantly, the violin concerto ended in a crescendo.'' See Chapter 9.

dangling participle   A participle serving as a modifier that has no word in the sentence for it to modify: "Looking out the window, a car drove by.'' See Chapter 9.

declarative sentence: A sentence that states a fact or makes a statement: "The capital of Kentucky is Frankfort.''

demonstrative pronoun: A word used as an adjective or a pronoun to point out an item referred to. The demonstrative pronouns are *this, that, these,* and *those.*

dependent clause   A group of words containing a subject and verb but unable to stand alone. A dependent clause must be subordinated to an independent clause in the same sentence: *"If you are on the honor roll,* you may be eligible for reduced insurance rates.'' See Chapter 7.

direct object   A word that receives the action of the verb: "She helped *him* with the math problem." "I pried the *lid* off the can." See Chapter 4.

elliptical construction   A construction in which one or more words are omitted but understood: "He is heavier than I *(am)*."

essential modifier   A word or group of words necessary for the identification of the object being identified: "The man *with the checkered vest* wants to talk to you." Essential modifiers can be words, phrases, or clauses; they are not separated from the words they modify by commas. See Chapter 10.

exclamatory sentence   A sentence expressing emotion, usually followed by an exclamation point: "Stop that chatter!"

formal language   Language appropriate to formal situations and occasions, as distinguished from informal language and colloquialisms.

fragment   See *sentence fragment.*

fused sentences   See *run-on sentence.*

gender   The grammatical expression of sex, particularly in the choice of pronouns: *he* (masculine), *she* (feminine), and *it* (neuter), and their related forms.

gerund   The *-ing* form of a verb when it is used as a noun: "*Jogging* is one of the most popular forms of exercise among Americans in the 1980s."

helping verb   See *auxiliary verb.*

imperative sentence   A sentence expressing a command: "Please turn off your motor."

indefinite pronoun   A pronoun that does not refer to a specific person or thing. Some of the most common indefinite pronouns include *anyone, someone, few, many,* and *none.* See Chapters 4 and 5.

independent clause   A group of words containing a subject and a verb and capable of standing alone. See Chapters 2 and 7.

indirect object   The person or thing receiving the direct object, and usually placed in a sentence between an action verb and the direct object: "Jay's lawyer gave *him* several documents to sign."

infinitive   The form of the verb preceded by *to: to hesitate, to think, to start,* etc.

informal language   Language appropriate to informal situations and occasions. Informal language often uses contractions and colloquialisms.

intensive pronouns   Pronouns that end in *-self* or *-selves* and emphasize their antecedents: *myself, yourself, himself, ourselves,* and so on. See Chapter 4.

interjection   A word or phrase expressing emotion but having no grammatical relationship to the other words in the sentence. Interjections include the following: *Yes, no, oh, well,* and so on. See Chapter 1.

interrogative pronoun   A pronoun that is used to form a question: *who, whom, what, which, whose.* "*Who* wants to play backgammon?"

intransitive verb   A verb that does not require an object: "They slept." See *transitive verb.*

inverted order   A sentence which is not in the usual word order of *subject-verb-object.* "Angry and dejected was he." See Chapter 2.

irregular verb   A verb that forms its past tense or past participle by changing its spelling: *bring* (brought); *think* (thought); *run* (ran). See Chapter 6 and *regular verb.*

linking verb   A verb that connects a subject in a sentence with another word (usually a noun, pronoun, or adjective) that renames or describes the subject. "The bacon *was* crisp." "You *seem* bored." See Chapters 1 and 4.

main clause   See *independent clause.*

mass noun   A noun referring to something usually measured by weight, degree, or volume rather than by count. Mass nouns are words like *assistance* (we don't say *one assistance, two assistances,* and so on), *money,* and *height.*

misplaced modifier   A word or group of words misplaced in the sentence and therefore modifying the wrong word: "I watched the parade standing on the balcony." See Chapter 9.

modifier   A word or group of words describing or modifying the meaning of another word in the sentence.

nonessential modifier   A word or group of words modifying a noun or pronoun but not essential to the meaning of the sentence. Nonessential modifiers are set off by commas: "My father, *who was born in Illinois,* was a metallurgical accountant." See Chapter 10.

noun   A word that names a person, place, thing, or idea. See Chapter 1.

noun clause   A dependent clause functioning as a subject, direct object, predicate nominative, or indirect object in a sentence: "He told me *what I wanted to hear.*"

number   The form of a word that indicates one *(singular)* or more than one *(plural).* See Chapters 3 and 11.

object   A word or group of words receiving the action of or affected by an action verb or a preposition. See *direct object, indirect object,* and *object of preposition.*

object of preposition   A word or group of words following a preposition and related to another part of the sentence by the preposition: "Vince drove his motorcycle across *the United States.*" See Chapter 1.

participle   The *-ing* form of a verb (the *present participle*) when it is used as an adjective (a *swimming* pool), or the *-d, -ed, -t,* or *-n* form of a verb (the *past participle)* when it is used as an adjective (the *painted* house).

past participle   See *participle.*

person   The form of a pronoun or verb used to show the speaker (*first person:* I am), the person spoken to (*second person:* you are), or the person spoken about (*third person:* she is). See Chapter 5.

personal pronoun   A pronoun that changes its form to show person: *I, you, he, she, they,* and so on.

phrase   A group of words lacking both a subject and a verb.

plural   More than one. See *number.*

positive degree   The form of the adjective or adverb which makes no comparison: *heavy* (positive degree); *heavier* (comparative degree); *heaviest* (superlative degree). See *comparative degree* and *superlative degree.*

possessive pronouns   Pronouns that show ownership: *my, mine, your, yours, his, her, hers, its, our,* and so on. See Chapters 1 and 4.

predicate   The verb, its modifiers, and any objects in a sentence. The predicate makes a statement about the subject of the sentence.

predicate adjective   An adjective that follows a linking verb and modifies the subject: "We were *happy* to get the news." See Chapter 1.

predicate noun   A noun that follows a linking verb and names the subject: "Harry is the *captain* of the lacrosse team."

predicate pronoun   A pronoun that follows a linking verb and identifies the subject: "My closest friend is *you.*" See Chapter 4.

preposition   A word that shows a relationship between its object and another word in the sentence. Common prepositions include *at, to, behind, below, for, among, with,* and so on. See Chapter 1.

prepositional phrase   A preposition and its object: *on the table, above the clouds, for the evening,* and so on. See Chapter 1.

present participle   See *participle.*

pronoun   A word that takes the place of a noun or another pronoun. See Chapters 1, 4, and 5.

pronoun form   The form of a pronoun based on its use. Pronouns change their forms when they are used as subjects, objects, or to show possession. See *case* and Chapter 4.

pronoun antecedent   See *antecedent* and Chapter 5.

pronoun reference   See *antecedent* and Chapter 5.

proper adjective   An adjective formed from a proper noun: *Italian* painting, *African* nations, *Irish* whiskey. Proper adjectives are usually capitalized except in phrases like "china cabinet" or "french fries."

proper noun   A noun referring to a specific person, place, or thing. Proper nouns are capitalized: *Denver; Mr. McAuliffe; Taj Mahal.* See Chapter 1.

reflexive pronoun   A pronoun ending in *-self* or *-selves* and renaming the subject.

Reflexive pronouns are objects of verbs and prepositions; "He perjured *himself*." "They went by *themselves*." See Chapter 4.

regular verb   A verb that forms its past tense by adding *-d*, or *-ed: start, started; hope, hoped.* See *irregular verb* and Chapter 6.

relative pronoun   A pronoun that introduces an adjective clause. The relative pronouns are *who, whom, whose, which, that.*

restrictive modifier   See *essential modifier.*

run-on sentence   Two independent clauses run together with no punctuation to separate them: "Her uncle works as a plumber in Des Moines he used to be a professor of philosophy in Boston." The run-on sentence is corrected by placing a semicolon or a comma and coordinate conjunction between the two clauses. See Chapter 8.

sentence   A group of words containing a subject and a verb and expressing some sense of completeness. See Chapter 2.

sentence fragment   A group of words lacking an independent clause and therefore unable to stand alone. See Chapter 8.

sentence types   Sentences classified on the basis of their structure. There are four types of sentences in English: simple, compound, complex, and compound-complex. See *simple, compound, complex, compound-complex,* and Chapter 7.

simple sentence   A sentence containing one independent clause.

slang   An informal word or expression not accepted in formal writing by careful or educated users of the language. Slang is usually short lived or temporary, and should be used sparingly.

split infinitive   An infinitive with a modifier between the *to* and the verb. Split infinitives are avoided by most careful speakers and writers. Some examples: *to really want; to hardly hear.*

squinting modifier   A modifier that makes the meaning of a sentence ambiguous because it modifies two words at the same time: "We stood around *nervously* waiting to be introduced"; "I asked them *politely* to leave." See Chapter 9.

standard English   The English of careful and educated speakers and writers.

subject   The part of the sentence about which the predicate makes a statement. See *predicate* and Chapter 2.

subordinate clause   See *dependent clause.*

subordinate conjunction   A word that joins a dependent clause to an independent clause. See Chapters 1 and 7.

superlative degree   The *most, least,* or *-est* form of those adjectives and adverbs that can be compared: *most beautiful; least valid; greatest.* See *comparative degree, comparison,* and *positive degree.*

tense   The form of a verb which shows the action as being in the past, present, or future times. The most common tenses are simple present, present perfect, simple past, past perfect, simple future, and future perfect. See Chapter 6.

transitive verb   A verb that requires an object in order to complete its meaning: "We *saw* the accident." "They *helped* their neighbors." See *intransitive verb*.

verb   A part of speech which describes the action or state of being of a subject. See Chapters 1 and 6.

Index

Index